THE

Gourmet

COOKIE BOOK

THE
Gourmet
COOKIE BOOK

The Single Best Recipe from Each Year 1941–2009

Houghton Mifflin Harcourt
Boston / New York

For information about permission to reproduce selections from this book,
write to Permissions, Houghton Mifflin Harcourt Publishing Company
215 Park Avenue South, New York, New York 10003.

www.hmhbooks.com

Library of Congress Cataloging-in-Publication Data
The Gourmet cookie book: the single best recipe from each year 1941–2009
p. cm.
ISBN 978-0-547-32816-4
1. Cookies I. Gourmet
TX 772.G68 2010
641.8'654—dc22   2010018882

For permissions, see page 161.

Book design by Richard Ferretti and Kevin DeMaria

Printed in the United States of America

DOC 10 9 8 7 6

ACKNOWLEDGMENTS

Although we had always treasured our cookie recipes, it took a few people who were relatively new to *Gourmet* to realize what an extraordinary resource we possessed. Web editors Adam Houghtaling and Christy Harrison and special projects editor Jacqueline Terrebonne came up with the idea of featuring the best cookie from each year of the magazine's existence. It was not until executive food editor Kemp Minifie began trolling through the archives that we really understood that this was more than a fabulous collection of cookies; it also told a very American story. It was no accident that every one of us found excuses to spend time in the kitchen while test kitchen director Ruth Cousineau—who threw herself, body and soul, into baking the cookies—was immersed in the project. These cookies are not only delicious; they are also a fascinating window into history that none of us wanted to miss.

Wonderful as these cookies were all by themselves, it took the passion and inspiration of creative director Richard Ferretti, associate art director Kevin DeMaria, and photographer Romulo Yanes to make them dance. Their vision has made this book a delight to look at.

We could not have done it without the help of former food editor Shelley Wiseman, who retested the cookies a final time. And when editors Rux Martin, Roy Finamore, and Judith Sutton came into the project, they asked demanding questions and lent it an entirely new life.

Thanks, too, to copy editor John Haney; nothing escaped his eagle eye. Research chief Marisa Robertson-Textor made certain that all our facts were correct, and when executive editor John Willoughby and senior articles editor Jane Daniels Lear gave the copy a final read, they each added their own important insights.

But in the end, this book would not have been possible without *Gourmet*'s devoted readers, who sent their cookies, their recipes, and their comments, for so many years. This book belongs to you, and we thank you for it.

CONTENTS

1976   1981   1986   1991   1996   2001   2006

1977   1982   1987   1992   1997   2002   2007

1978   1983   1988   1993   1998   2003   2008

1979   1984   1989   1994   1999   2004   2009

1980   1985   1990   1995   2000   2005

THE BASICS

CONTENTS

78
1976
LEMON THINS

90
1981
CLOUDT'S
PECAN TREATS

100
1986
PASTELITOS DE
BODA

112
1991
JAN HAGELS

122
1996
ANISE-SCENTED
FIG AND DATE
SWIRLS

134
2001
CRANBERRY
TURTLE BARS

144
2006
CHOCOLATE
PEPPERMINT
BAR COOKIES

80
1977
IRISH COFFEE
CRUNCHIES

92
1982
CHOCOLATE
MERINGUE
BISCUITS

102
1987
MOCHA TOFFEE
BARS

114
1992
CRANBERRY
PISTACHIO
BISCOTTI

124
1997
CHOCOLATE
COCONUT
SQUARES

136
2002
SCANDINAVIAN
ROSETTES

146
2007
TRIOS

82
1978
BIZCOCHITOS

94
1983
SWITZ

104
1988
PISTACHIO
TUILES

116
1993
AUNT SIS'S
STRAWBERRY
TART COOKIES

126
1998
GIANDUIA
BROWNIES

138
2003 BISCOTTI
QUADRATI AL
MIELE E ALLE
NOCI

148
2008 GLITTERING
LEMON
SANDWICH
COOKIES

84
1979
LINZER BARS

96
1984
SOUVAROFFS

106
1989
CORNETTI

118
1994
BASLER BRUNSLI

128
1999
SKIBO CASTLE
GINGER CRUNCH

140
2004
POLISH APRICOT-
FILLED COOKIES

150
2009
GRAND MARNIER
GLAZED PAIN
D´EPICE COOKIES

88
1980
BOURBON BALLS

98
1985
PECAN TASSIES

110
1990
MOCHA
COOKIES

120
1995
COCONUT
MACADAMIA
SHORTBREAD

132
2000
WALNUT ACORN
COOKIES

142
2005
MINI BLACK
AND WHITE
COOKIES

152
THE
BASICS

INTRODUCTION

Buy a cookie, and it's just a bite of sugar, something sweet to get you through the day. Bake a cookie, on the other hand, and you send an instant message from the moment you measure out the flour. Long before they're done, the cookies become a promise, their endlessly soothing scent offering both reassurance and solace. And even the tiniest bite is powerful, bringing with it the flavor of home. For anyone who is comfortable in a kitchen, a warm cookie is the easiest way to say I love you.

Somewhere in the back of our minds, we all know this. It is the reason we bake cookies at Christmas, why we exchange them as gifts. Not for nothing do we pack up our cookies and send them off to our far-flung families. Like little ambassadors of good will, these morsels stand in for us. There are few people who don't understand, at least subconsciously, how much a cookie can mean.

But until we began work on this book, it had never occurred to us to look at history through a cookie prism. When we decided to select the best cookie from each of

Gourmet's sixty-eight years, we knew we would end up with an awesome array of treats. But we did not realize that we would also discover a way of charting the changes in the way that we eat. Our cookie cravings, it turns out, offer a fascinating window on history, a portrait of our country that reveals the way our appetites have evolved.

We were so captivated by the language of cookies that we have printed the recipes exactly as they originally appeared. In the early years, they are remarkably casual, a kind of mysterious shorthand that assumes that each reader is an accomplished cook who needs very little in the way of guidance. "Bake in a moderate oven until crisp," is a classic instruction. So is "Add flour until the dough is stiff." It's interesting to watch as numbers creep into the recipes in the form of degrees, minutes, and cups. And it's startling to observe the recipes growing longer and longer as they become increasingly precise.

Although we have left the language of the recipes unchanged, we have removed the guesswork; when we retested, we added notes, so that you'll know exactly how hot your oven should be, and how many cups of flour it takes to stiffen that dough.

Cookies turn out to be an excellent indicator of what we have been eating. The instinct to bake them is essentially conservative, which means that cookies are rarely the first place that new ingredients appear. An ingredient must have a solid place at America's table before it makes its way into the cookie cupboard. So when pistachios start showing up in cookies in the eighties, you know that the luxurious nut has finally become part of the American food landscape. And when, in the early nineties, espresso stops making the occasional appearance and turns into a standard ingredient, it is no accident; this is just when *venti* became part of our vocabulary, a sign that America's drinking habits had undergone a serious revolution.

Looking at cookies in this way is a fascinating exercise. It is also a great predictor of future trends. Work your way through this book and you'll be in a very good position to know what cookies we'll be baking next year, and the year after that. But while new cookies keep being invented, old cookies never die. They just get better and better. We like to think that you'll be baking the ones in this book for many years to come.

—THE EDITORS

RECIPE TIPS

INGREDIENTS

All ingredients should be at room temperature unless otherwise specified.

→ Butter: Use unsalted butter unless otherwise specified. Always allow butter to soften before beating it; beating is often called "creaming."

→ Sugar: Most of these recipes use granulated white sugar. Do not substitute another kind, as your results may be different.

→ Eggs: Use large eggs. Eggs can be separated more easily when they are cold, but they should be brought to room temperature before you add them to a dough. To do this quickly, put them in a bowl of cold water for 15 minutes.

→ Salt: Use table salt unless otherwise specified. Do not leave out the salt; it brings out the sweetness and flavor of the other ingredients.

→ Molasses: Use ordinary molasses; robust molasses can add a bitter flavor.

MEASURING

Measure liquids in glass or clear plastic liquid-measuring cups.

→ Measure dry ingredients in nesting dry-measuring cups so they can be leveled off with a knife.

→ Measure flour by spooning it into a dry-measuring cup (not by scooping it directly from the flour with the dry measure). Level it off with a knife; do not tap or shake the cup.

→ Do not sift flour unless specified in the recipe. If sifted flour is called for, sift before measuring the flour. (Disregard "presifted" on the label.)

→ Measure brown sugar by packing it into a dry-measuring cup.

→ Store spices away from heat and light; buy them in small quantities.

→ Toast whole spices in a dry heavy skillet over medium heat, stirring, until fragrant and a shade darker, 3 to 5 minutes.

→ Toast nuts on a baking sheet in a 350°F oven until golden, 5 to 15 minutes, depending on the type of nut.

→ Toast seeds as you would spices or nuts.

→ Grind nuts just until loose and crumbly; do not grind them to a paste. If using a food processor, use the pulse button rather than processing the nuts to a paste. If the nuts have been toasted, let them cool before grinding.

→ Melt chocolate in a metal bowl set over a saucepan of barely simmering water, stirring occasionally. Or microwave at low to medium power for short intervals (30 seconds or less; stir after each interval to check the consistency).

→ To zest citrus, remove only the colored part of the rind; avoid the bitter white pith. For grated zest, we prefer a Microplane, a rasp grater, which results in fluffier zest;

if using a Microplane, pack the zest into the measuring spoon when measuring. For strips of zest, use a vegetable peeler.

EQUIPMENT

We prefer medium-weight, light-colored baking pans, not nonstick. (If you do use dark metal pans, including nonstick, your cookies may brown more, and the cooking times may be shorter; lower the oven temperature 25°F to compensate.) For cookie baking, we prefer the baking sheets, often called cookie sheets, that have only one or two lipped sides for easier handling, allowing you to slide the cookies quickly and easily from the pan to the cooling rack. We are not fans of insulated cookie sheets, because cookies tend to take longer to bake on them. If you bake cookies often, it's best to have at least two cookie sheets. When baking batches of cookies, be sure the pans have cooled before you place more dough on them. A warm pan will cause the cookies to spread too much.

TECHNIQUES

Rolling: Don't add more flour than necessary to the work surface when rolling out the dough, or the cookies may be tough. If rolling the dough into balls in the palms of your hands to make the cookies, wet your hands slightly to prevent the dough from sticking.

Cutting: Dip cookie cutters in flour before cutting out cookies, to prevent the dough from sticking. Then remove the scraps from around each cookie, lift the cookie with a spatula, and place it on the baking sheet. → Chilling cookies on the baking sheet after cutting them will help them keep their shape during baking.

Spacing: Place the cookies on the cookie sheet about 2 inches apart unless otherwise specified.

Cooling: Let the cookies cool on the baking sheet for a minute or two, unless otherwise specified, before transferring them to a wire rack to cool completely.

BUTTER EQUIVALENTS

Volume	Sticks	Weight
¼ cup	½ stick	2 ounces
6 Tbs.	¾ stick	3 ounces
½ cup	1 stick	¼ pound
¾ cup	1½ sticks	6 ounces
1 cup	2 sticks	½ pound
1¼ cups	1½ sticks	10 ounces
1½ cups	3 sticks	¾ pound
1¾ cups	1½ sticks	14 ounces
2 cups	4 sticks	1 pound

1940s

1941 was an unlikely time to launch an epicurean magazine. War was looming, along with the possibility of food rationing. But *Gourmet*'s founder, Earle MacAusland, convinced that soldiers who had spent time in Europe and Asia would be loath to come back to meat loaf, saw an opportunity. Little wonder then that *Gourmet*, published from a penthouse at the Plaza Hotel, concentrated on sophisticated fare. Cookies did not figure into the equation, and the few recipes that the magazine published leaned toward old-fashioned American classics like wafers and sugar crisps, with a couple of European treats.

CAJUN MACAROONS

America's first epicurean magazine had very ambitious plans. Although war was imminent, you wouldn't have known it from turning the pages. In this, the second issue, *Gourmet*'s chef, Louis P. DeGouy ("de *goo*-ey"), taught his readers how to cook a duck. They could also read about "Famous Chefs of Today"; peruse the first installment of "Clementine in the Kitchen," the story of a French cook (the series eventually became a beloved book); and shop vicariously at a store that specialized in dates (it sold Deglet Noors, Golden Saidys, and black Hyanas). Turning to the menus, they found a rather elaborate celebration of Mardi Gras in New Orleans, complete with oysters rockefeller, Creole soup, papaya balls, pompano fillets, pigeon pie, poinsettia salad (canned pineapple, pimiento strips, cream cheese moistened with French dressing, and paprika), creamed peas, and sugared yams.

But the best thing about the menu was the finale: crisp, chewy little cookies with a subtle almond scent. Although the recipe required a lot of work, readers would beg for it again and again over the years. Happily, the food processor has taken most of the labor out of these French-style macaroons, and today they are a breeze to make.

MAKES ABOUT 4 DOZEN 1½-INCH COOKIES

These should be baked a few days in advance. They will keep several months when kept in a closed tin in a cool, dry place.

Work **½ pound almond paste** with a wooden spoon until it is smooth. Add **3 slightly beaten egg whites** and blend thoroughly. Add **½ cup sifted pastry flour**, resifted with **½ cup fine granulated sugar** and **½ cup powdered sugar**. Cover a cooky sheet or sheets with bond paper. The cooky mixture may be dropped from the tip of a teaspoon and shaped on the paper, or may be pressed through a cooky press, or shaped with a pastry bag and tube. Bake in a slow oven (300°F) about 30 minutes. The cakes may be removed from the paper by means of a spatula while still warm.

VARIATIONS: Finely chopped or ground candied fruits may be added to the mixture before baking. Or the tops of the macaroons may be decorated before baking by placing in the center of each a nut half, a raisin (seedless, black or white), or a bit of candied fruit—such as a bit of angelica—cut fancifully, or by sprinkling with finely chopped nut meats. The cakes may be decorated after baking by dainty frosting designs formed with the help of a cake decorator or a pastry tube.

RECIPE NOTES
1. The almond paste should be at room temperature.
2. Rather than working the almond paste with a wooden spoon, use a food processor.
3. Use White Lily flour (see Sources, page 154) or cake flour (not self-rising) in place of the pastry flour.
4. Use regular granulated sugar in place of fine granulated sugar.
5. In place of the bond paper that the recipe calls for, use parchment paper.
6. The cookies should be pale golden.

HONEY REFRIGERATOR COOKIES

The war was on, and sugar was rationed. Aiming to do its patriotic bit, *Gourmet* printed an article showing readers how to use honey in place of sugar. The author of the article considered the shortage of sugar a good thing, harrumphing that until the discovery of sugar refining in the middle of the eighteenth century, cooks were very happy to rely on honey. He expressed the hope that "with the present curtailment in our sugar supply, honey will regain much of its former glory." That desire is probably why these cookies are so good; delicate and barely sweet, they are almost biscuit-like and go well with cheese. They also improve immeasurably with age.

In a sign of the times, the recipe ran next to a cartoon of a woman emerging from a car in front of a fancy restaurant, peering at the 30-minute parking sign and saying to her husband, "Sometimes I think you park in these restricted areas so we won't have time to order the deluxe dinner."

MAKES ABOUT 80 COOKIES

Cream together **½ cup each of honey, brown sugar**, and **shortening**. Beat in **1 egg**; then add **2½ cups flour** sifted with **1 teaspoon baking powder**, **¼ teaspoon soda**, **½ teaspoon salt**, and **½ cup nut meats**. Shape the dough into a roll or loaf, or press it into refrigerator cookie molds. Allow the dough to ripen for a day or two in the refrigerator before you slice and bake it in a hot oven (400°F) for 10 to 12 minutes.

RECIPE NOTES
1. The shortening should be at room temperature before beating.
2. "Soda" is baking soda.
3. Use ½ cup coarsely chopped walnuts.
4. Instead of pressing the cookies into molds, roll the dough into 2-inch-diameter rectangular logs, then slice and bake.

SCOTCH OAT CRUNCHIES

During the war, *Gourmet* staffers—and everybody else—tried many tricks with oatmeal. We're not so fond of the oatmeal macaroons the editors concocted for the article on "The King's Porridge," and we have definite reservations about their haggis recipe. But these sandwich cookies are an entirely different matter. They have a slightly nutty flavor and an appealingly crumbly texture, and they are extremely forgiving: fill them with your jam of choice. No matter what you choose, they taste wonderful.

MAKES ABOUT 4 DOZEN COOKIES

These can be filled with dates, raisins, mincemeat, figs, apricots, or what you will.

→ Cream **1 cup butter** until it is almost white; gradually add **1 cup light brown sugar**, and keep on creaming until the two are thoroughly blended. Combine **2½ cups pastry flour** and **½ teaspoon each of baking powder** and **salt**; sift twice into a dry mixing bowl. Stir in **2½ cups rolled oats**. When this mixture is thoroughly blended, add to it alternately the creamed butter and **½ cup cold water** to which has been added **2 or 3 drops almond extract** and **¼ teaspoon vanilla extract**. Chill for at least 25 minutes.

→ Roll out a portion of the dough about ⅛ inch thick, or as thin as it can be rolled on a slightly floured board. Cut into rounds about 2 inches in diameter; lift these with a broad spatula onto a generously buttered baking sheet, and bake for 10 minutes in a moderate oven (350°F), or until the cookies are slightly browned. Cool and store in a cookie jar. They will keep indefinitely in a cool, dry place. When ready to use, spread a filling on one cookie and top it with another, and eat immediately.

RECIPE NOTES

1. The butter should be softened before beating (creaming).
2. Use White Lily flour (see Sources, page 154) or cake flour (not self-rising) instead of the pastry flour.
3. Because the dough contains a generous amount of butter, chill it overnight to make it easier to roll out.
4. A tart filling like sour cherry jam brings out the cookies' best.

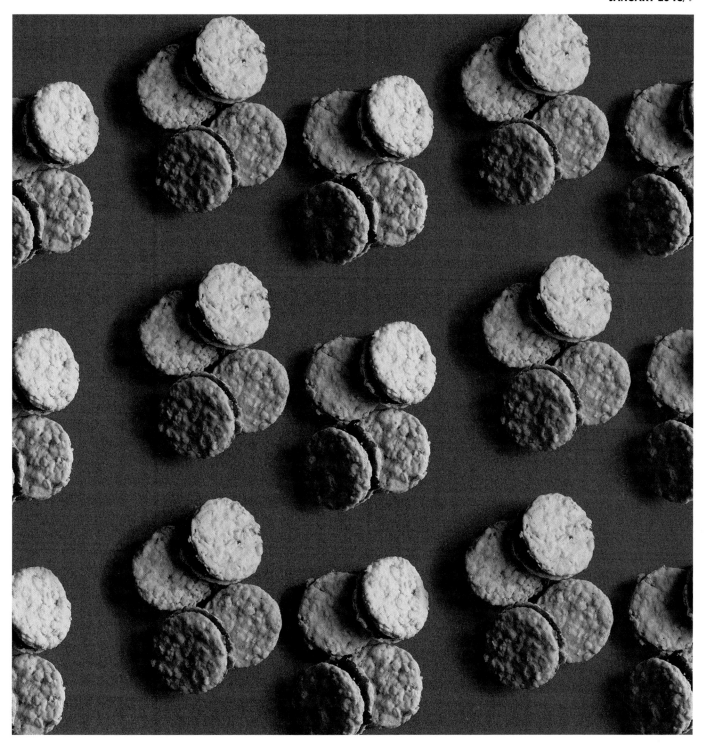

CINNAMON SUGAR CRISPS

In her column "Food Flashes," the influential food writer Clementine Paddleford extolled the virtues of a new popover mix called Puff-Over, which sold for 41 cents. *Gourmet* advised readers on what to put in the parcels they were sending to their boys in the army. And for the first time, the editors created an entire column called "Cookie Jar," offering the opportunity to fill those packages with homemade treats. Sugar was still rationed, and everyone was eager to send great cookies overseas, so every single recipe had to be special. We like them all, but these thin spice cookies are our favorites because, although they are simple to make, they are stunningly crisp and light.

MAKES ABOUT 4 DOZEN COOKIES

Cream **½ cup butter or margarine** with **¾ cup granulated sugar** until the mixture is light and lemon colored; and continuing the creaming, add first **1 large well-beaten egg**, then **⅔ cup molasses** flavored with **½ teaspoon vanilla extract** and **¼ teaspoon almond extract**. Sift together **2½ cups pastry flour** with **1 teaspoon baking powder**, **2 generous teaspoons powdered cinnamon**, **½ teaspoon soda**, and a **generous ½ teaspoon salt**. Add the flour mixture gradually to the creamed butter and molasses, mixing well after each addition. When the dough is well blended, pat it out first on a floured board, then roll it to ⅛ inch in thickness. Cut it with a small floured cookie cutter, and arrange the cookies on an ungreased baking sheet. Bake them in a moderate oven (350°F) for about 10 to 12 minutes, or until crisp. Before the baking, the tops of the cookies may be moistened with milk, water, or fruit juice and then sprinkled with mixed sugar and cinnamon. When the cookies are cold, store them in a tightly closed jar, and keep in a cool, dry place.

RECIPE NOTES
1. We use butter, not margarine, for the best flavor.
2. Use White Lily flour (see Sources, page 154) or cake flour (not self-rising) in place of the pastry flour.
3. "Soda" is baking soda.
4. The dough will be soft, so it is important to chill it, wrapped well, for at least 3 hours, or overnight, before rolling it out.
5. Use a well-floured board and floured rolling pin when rolling out the dough.
6. The cookies will stick to ungreased cookie sheets; line them with parchment paper, and the cookies will release easily.

DATE BARS

We chose this recipe for two reasons. First, because it was the first postwar cookie to appear in *Gourmet,* which makes it momentous. And second, because it is so delicious. The recipe appeared in one of many articles about Katish, a remarkable Russian cook who had a great many fans. "I think I've copied every one of her recipes as they've appeared," wrote M. F. K. Fisher in an appreciative note. Katish, who worked for an almost comically typical California family, was enamored of all things American. In this installment, she got her first electric refrigerator and was so thrilled with it that she went on a mad cooking binge. She started with shashlik (skewers of lamb) and her special hot chocolate and ended with these easy cookies. Moist, chewy, and quite sweet, they will remind you of something your grandmother might have made.

MAKES 3 DOZEN BARS

Crumble **14 graham crackers** fine and mix with **½ teaspoon salt** and **1½ teaspoons baking powder**. Add **1¾ cups chopped dates** and **1 cup broken walnut meats**. Beat **3 eggs** well and gradually add **1 cup brown sugar**, then beat in the first mixture. Pour into a well-greased square pan and bake 20 to 25 minutes at 375°F. Cut while warm and toss in powdered sugar.

RECIPE NOTES
1. Use 1¼ cups graham cracker crumbs.
2. Use a 9-inch square baking pan. Grease the baking pan with butter, line it with two crisscrossed sheets of foil, and butter the foil.
3. Make 36 squares by cutting the bars into 6 rows each lengthwise and crosswise.

MORAVIAN WHITE CHRISTMAS COOKIES

A whole piglet stretched across the cover. He had an apple in his mouth and was wrapped in a wreath of holly. Inside articles extolled potent punch and the joys of smoking cigars. ("A gourmet without a cigar at the end of his major meal is like an unfortunate who has only one leg. He is to be pitied, for he merely hops along in the world of gastronomy.") As if to make up for the male bent of the issue, the editors included a sweet little article about growing up in the Moravian community of Bethlehem, Pennsylvania. It contained an unusual recipe for the thin, gently spicy classic Christmas cookie. Although most Moravian cookies are dark, this one is very pale. We particularly like its lovely flavor of mingled cinnamon, nutmeg, and sherry. While it is stable and strong enough for decorating, it remains light, crisp, and very delicious.

MAKES ABOUT 6 DOZEN COOKIES

Cream **1 cup butter**, add **2 cups sugar** gradually, and cream the mixture until it is light. Add **4 well-beaten eggs** and beat the whole thoroughly. Sift **3 cups flour** with **½ teaspoon salt**, **½ teaspoon cinnamon**, and **¼ teaspoon nutmeg**, and add it alternately with **2 tablespoons sherry**. Add sufficient **flour, 1 cup**, to stiffen the dough. Chill for several hours.
→ Roll the chilled dough extremely thin and cut it out with cookie cutters in star, diamond, or heart shapes. Put them on a greased baking sheet and bake in a hot oven (450°F) for about 7 minutes.

RECIPE NOTES
1. The butter should be softened before beating (creaming).
2. Roll out the dough to 1⁄16 inch thick.
3. The original recipe did not include an icing. To decorate, see page 152.

OLD-FASHIONED CHRISTMAS BUTTER COOKIES

By 1947, memories of the war were beginning to recede and the country had relaxed into a more lighthearted mood. That's evident from the cover, which boasted a Christmas tree with gifts piled beneath it. Inside were stories about "Truffles and Trifles," "Gilding the Goose," and, for the first time ever, an article about gingerbread men. As if slightly embarrassed by such frivolity, the editors also included these cookies, which they insisted on calling the "pride of the thrifty housewife." That is definitely underselling them. The cookies are made with modest ingredients, and they keep for weeks, but we were taken with the old-fashioned technique, which calls for blending sieved hard-cooked yolks and raw yolks into the dough, and then perfuming it with lemon zest or a dash of brandy. What you end up with are cookies that are incredibly crisp and so flaky they almost seem to float away.

MAKES ABOUT 12 DOZEN COOKIES

Put **3 hard-cooked yolks** through a fine sieve. Cream **1 pound (2 cups) sweet butter** and gradually add **1½ cups sugar**, stirring constantly until light and fluffy. Add the 3 strained yolks alternately with **6 cups sifted flour** and **3 raw yolks**. Knead the mixture with your hands until thoroughly blended, or until the dough is smooth and easily handled. Add the **rind of ½ lemon or 2 teaspoons brandy** and continue kneading.

· Chill the dough several hours, then roll as thin as possible. Cut it with cookie cutters in as many fancy shapes as desired. Brush each cookie very evenly with **slightly beaten white of egg**. Sprinkle the tops with a mixture of **1 cup each sugar** and **blanched almonds or walnuts**, coarsely chopped. Place them on a slightly floured cooky sheet and bake in a moderate oven (350°F) for 10 to 15 minutes, or until delicately brown, removing each cooky as it is ready.

RECIPE NOTES

1. To hard-cook eggs, put them in a saucepan with cold water to cover, partially cover pan, and bring the water to a rolling boil, reduce the heat to low, and cook the eggs for 30 seconds. Remove from the heat and let stand in the water, covered, for 15 minutes, then run under cold water for about 5 minutes.
2. The butter should be softened before beating (creaming).
3. Use grated lemon zest (without any of the bitter white pith).
4. Roll out the dough to a ⅟₁₆-inch thickness.
5. Instead of flouring the sheets, line them with parchment paper.

JELLY CENTERS

America was finally starting to feel prosperous. The menu for a June anniversary party boasted dishes that were both luxurious and pretty. The table was resplendent with molded salads garnished with radish roses, decorated cold salmon, lobster en croûte, light chicken mousse, cottage-cheese hearts topped with strawberries, and plates of dainty little petits fours. These cookies were no exception. Rich with egg yolks, strewn with chopped almonds, and filled with jewel-toned jams, they are exactly what you want when you're in the mood to pamper yourself.

MAKES ABOUT 11 DOZEN COOKIES

Cream **1 cup butter** until it is light. Add gradually **1 cup powdered or very fine granulated sugar**, creaming well after each addition. Add **6 egg yolks,** one at a time, **a pinch salt**, and the **juice and rind of ½ lemon**. Gradually add **3 cups sifted flour** and stir or knead the dough until thoroughly blended. Chill for at least 2 hours.
→ Roll the dough with slightly floured hands into uniform balls the size of large marbles. Press a slight indentation into each ball with your little finger. Paint with **beaten egg yolk** and sprinkle the tops with finely chopped **blanched almonds and sugar**. Bake in a moderate oven (350°F) until the balls are golden brown. When ready to serve, fill the indentations with **apricot jam or any red jams or jellies**.

RECIPE NOTES
1. The butter should be softened before beating (creaming).
2. We make the cookies with confectioners' (powdered) sugar.
3. Use grated lemon zest (without any of the bitter white pith).
4. Grease the baking sheets with butter.
5. The cookies will bake in about 12 minutes.

BRANDY SNAPS

These cookies are delightful—but they contain no brandy. A mistake? Not really. Although the English wafers called brandy snaps were originally made with spirits, bakers soon found that the liquor contributed very little in the way of taste or texture. It was so much less expensive to make virgin cookies that they began to leave the liquor out. Ultrathin, these cookies melt in the mouth and are perfect served with ice cream.

MAKES 18 TO 20 DOZEN COOKIES

Heat together in a saucepan **1½ cups each butter and sugar** and **1 cup molasses,** stirring the mixture until it is well blended. Stir in **4 teaspoons powdered ginger**, remove the pan from the heat, and add **3 cups sifted all-purpose flour**, a little at a time, beating well after each addition. Drop the batter from the tip of a spoon onto a buttered cooky sheet, allowing 2 inches between the wafers. Bake in a slow oven (300°F) for about 12 minutes, or until they are nicely browned. Remove from the pan immediately with a spatula and roll the wafers over a wooden stick or the handle of a wooden spoon. Or, if preferred, shape them into cones. Store the brandy snaps in airtight containers.

→ As a **VARIATION**, **1½ teaspoons grated lemon rind** may be added to the batter with the ginger.

RECIPE NOTES

1. Use about 2 teaspoons batter for each cookie.
2. For the variation, we used grated lemon zest (without any of the bitter white pith).
3. Be sure to remove the snaps from the baking sheet while they're still warm and immediately roll them around the handle of a wooden spoon or a wooden dowel.
4. Work with several cookies at once so you have time to shape them as they cool. Return the cookies to the oven for a few seconds if they cool and become hard to roll.
5. Brandy snaps not only keep well, they taste better on the second day.

1950s

Americans were feeling flush, and the women who had stepped in to keep the country going while the men were at war had been sent straight back to their kitchens. It was no coincidence that the number of cookie recipes in *Gourmet*'s pages doubled. Christmas cookies were an especially high-growth category, with recipes for gingerbread, Pfeffernüsse, shortbread, and spice cookies reappearing year after year. The magazine also published its first Italian cookie recipes in the 1950s, along with the other usual European suspects.

CHOCOLATE WAFERS

"Good cooks were pleasing their menfolks with chocolate cakes back during the early settling of the New England colonies . . . Modern ways are upon us, atom bombs bedevil our dreams, standardization of taste haunts our mealtimes—but chocolate is still chocolate." *Gourmet*'s article on chocolate (timed for Valentine's Day) offered all manner of cakes, tortes, soufflés, and pies, but only one cookie. With a chocolate wafer like this one—not too sweet, filled with flavor, and very sophisticated—who needs more? Crisp and thin, it is deeply, deeply chocolaty.

MAKES ABOUT 6 DOZEN COOKIES

Cream **¾ cup butter**, add gradually **1¼ cups sugar**, and cream them together until light and fluffy. Add **1 tablespoon rum extract** and **1 egg** to the butter-sugar mixture and beat thoroughly. Sift together **1½ cups sifted flour, ¾ cup breakfast cocoa, 1½ teaspoons double-action baking powder**, and **¼ teaspoon salt**. Add the sifted dry ingredients gradually, mixing well after each addition to make a light dough. Roll the dough out ⅛ inch in thickness on a lightly floured board and cut it with a floured cooky cutter into rounds about 2½ inches in diameter. Place the rounds on an ungreased baking sheet in a 375°F oven and bake for 8 minutes.

RECIPE NOTES
1. The butter should be softened before beating (creaming).
2. "Breakfast cocoa" is unsweetened cocoa.
3. To make for easy rolling, chill the dough until quite firm; overnight is best.

NAVETTES SUCRÉES (SUGAR SHUTTLES)

"Sugar shuttles?" we asked ourselves. It seemed too early to be a reference to space travel. In fact, it turns out that these cigar-shaped cookies resemble the device that holds the thread on a loom or sewing machine. These are a true taste of the past—crisp and shaggy on the outside, with a cake-like crumb. Although this old-fashioned cookie resembles nothing we'd seen before, it is definitely ready for a close-up and a comeback. Besides being a textural treat that melts in your mouth with an appealing sweetness, it looks spectacular on a cookie plate.

MAKES ABOUT 20 COOKIES

Sift **1 cup sifted all-purpose flour**, **¼ cup sugar**, and **¼ teaspoon salt** into a bowl. Add **¼ cup soft butter**, **2 egg yolks**, and **1 teaspoon vanilla** and knead until the dough is well blended. Chill it in the refrigerator for 2 hours.

→ Divide the dough into portions the size of a small walnut. Roll each piece of dough with the palm of the hand on a lightly floured board to give it the shape of a small sewing-machine shuttle. Dip each in **egg white** and roll in **granulated sugar**. Bake on a lightly buttered baking sheet in a moderate oven (350°F) for about 8 minutes, or until the little cookies are lightly browned.

RECIPE NOTES
1. Use unsalted butter.
2. The cylinder "shuttle" should be about 2½ inches long and ½ inch thick.
3. Lightly beat the egg white with a fork.

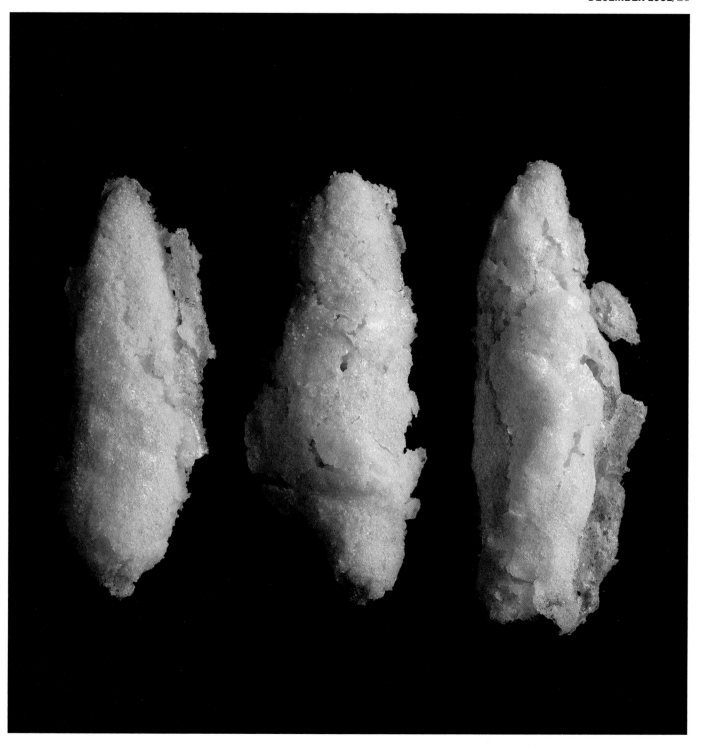

PALETS DE DAMES

Light and lovely, this cookie is a bit like a madeleine, with the addition of rum-soaked currants that lend it a uniquely heady touch. Its name refers to the French game of ringtoss, and the thin browned disks with browned rims recall the rope rings used in the game. The recipe comes from an article on *petits fours secs,* which, according to the text, are unlike *petits fours glacés* in that they are "sufficient unto themselves and scorn to depend upon butter and sugar icings for their enchantingly simple, enchantingly lovely taste and texture." *Gourmet* reprinted the instructions for this particular little confection over and over during the early years, and no wonder.

MAKES ABOUT 7 DOZEN COOKIES

Soak **4 tablespoons currants** in **2 tablespoons rum** for half an hour. Cream **1/2 cup butter** with **½ cup fine granulated sugar** until the mixture is light and fluffy. Beat in **2 eggs**, one at a time, and stir in **1 cup sifted flour** and the currants and rum. Put the batter into a pastry bag fitted with a large round tube and press mounds about the size of a half dollar onto a buttered and floured baking sheet. Bake the little cakes in a hot oven (450°F) for about 5 minutes, or until lightly browned. Remove the *palets de dames* to a cake rack to cool.

RECIPE NOTES
1. The butter should be softened before beating (creaming).
2. Use regular granulated sugar in place of the fine granulated sugar.
3. Use a ½-inch plain tip to pipe the cookies.
4. Be sure to give the cookies a lot of room on the baking sheet— about 2 inches apart; they will spread.
5. Bake the cookies for 6 to 7 minutes.

COCONUT BARS

The recipe list for the October issue included wild duck, young partridge with grapes, poached marrow, couscous, neck of lamb Grecque, feijoada, goose liver pies, and *petites bouchées*. Despite the sheer sophistication of the other offerings, *Gourmet*'s cooks responded to reader Miss Hope Austin's request for a recipe for cookies "made with coconut and sprinkled with powdered sugar that have cake-like bottoms and chewy tops," with these straightforward coconut bars. Studded with chopped walnuts and shredded coconut, they are like blondies with a tropical flair.

MAKES 2 DOZEN BARS

Cream **½ cup butter**. Add gradually **½ cup brown sugar** and beat until smooth. Stir in **1 cup sifted flour** and spread the batter in the bottom of an 8-inch square cake pan. Bake in a moderate oven (375°F) for 20 minutes.

→ Beat **2 eggs** and **1 cup light brown sugar** until smooth. Stir in **1 teaspoon vanilla**, **1 cup chopped walnuts**, and **½ cup shredded coconut** tossed with **2 tablespoons flour** and a **pinch of salt**. Spread this batter over the baked crust and continue to bake for 20 minutes longer. Cool, sprinkle with powdered sugar, and cut into squares or bars.

RECIPE NOTES
1. The butter should be softened before beating (creaming).
2. Butter the baking pan, line it with two crisscrossed sheets of foil, and then butter the foil.

BENNE WAFERS

Preparing for Christmas, *Gourmet*'s editors suggested a few mail-order gifts. These included: 6 live Maine lobsters, packed in seaweed and shipped in a free kettle ($9.92); a brace of Texas pheasants ($9); three 2-foot-long Louisiana sugarcanes ($1.99); a dozen sweet, stringless Colorado Pascal celery stalks "in a gay box" ($5.75); 3 Cornish pullets from the Danish humorist and musician Victor Borge, who bragged that his birds ate better than he did ($12.50); and 8 dozen fresh Long Island oysters in the shell ($5.50). If you wanted to offer your friends sweet benne wafers from South Carolina, however, the only option was to make them yourself. A tin of the thin, chewy, caramelized sesame-seed cookies ("benne" is an African word for "sesame"), with their stark nutty goodness, is a truly wonderful gift.

MAKES ABOUT 4 DOZEN COOKIES

Cream together **1½ tablespoons butter** and **1 cup light brown sugar** until light and smooth. Add **1 beaten egg**, **2 tablespoons flour**, **¼ teaspoon salt**, **1 teaspoon vanilla**, and **½ cup parched benne seeds**. Mix all together and drop from a teaspoon onto a buttered cooky sheet. Flatten the wafers with a knife dipped in ice water and bake in a moderate oven (350°F) for 6 minutes.

RECIPE NOTES
1. The butter should be softened before beating (creaming).
2. "Parched benne seeds" means sesame seeds.

BISCOTTI DI REGINA (QUEEN'S BISCUITS)

Gourmet's readers have always enjoyed sharing their recipes with fellow cooks. In 1955 an Alaskan offered a very long recipe for cooking seal, another reader sent in a recipe for steak cooked on ashes, and a Rhode Island doctor presented his recipe for boudin noir (it required a quart and a half of fresh pig's blood and a quarter teaspoon of garlic powder). Readers also wrote in with pleas for lost recipes; this issue fielded requests for creative ways to use a large pomegranate harvest, recipes for mock turtle soup, and an ice cream called Hokey Pokey, along with a poignant plea for "the cookies served at Italian weddings and christenings." To please the last writer, the editors came up with this classic, cake-like sesame cookie, which has been enjoyed in Italy for generations.

MAKES ABOUT 5 DOZEN BISCUITS

Cream **1 cup butter** and **1 cup sugar** until light and fluffy. Beat in **1 egg** and add gradually **½ cup milk** and **1 tablespoon vanilla extract**. Sift together into a bowl **5 cups flour**, **¾ teaspoon salt**, and **2 tablespoons double-action baking powder**. Make a hollow in the center and gradually work in the butter-sugar mixture. If the dough seems too dry, add more milk. Shape the dough into a ball and chill it in the refrigerator for at least 1 hour.

→ Wash and drain well **½ pound sesame seeds**. Break off pieces of the chilled dough the size of walnuts and flatten them slightly between the palms. Roll the biscuits in the sesame seeds and bake them on a cookie sheet ½ inch apart in a hot oven (450°F) for 10 to 12 minutes, or until golden.

RECIPE NOTES
1. The butter should be softened before beating (creaming).
2. Rinsing the sesame seeds helps them stick to the dough balls. You will need about 2 cups.

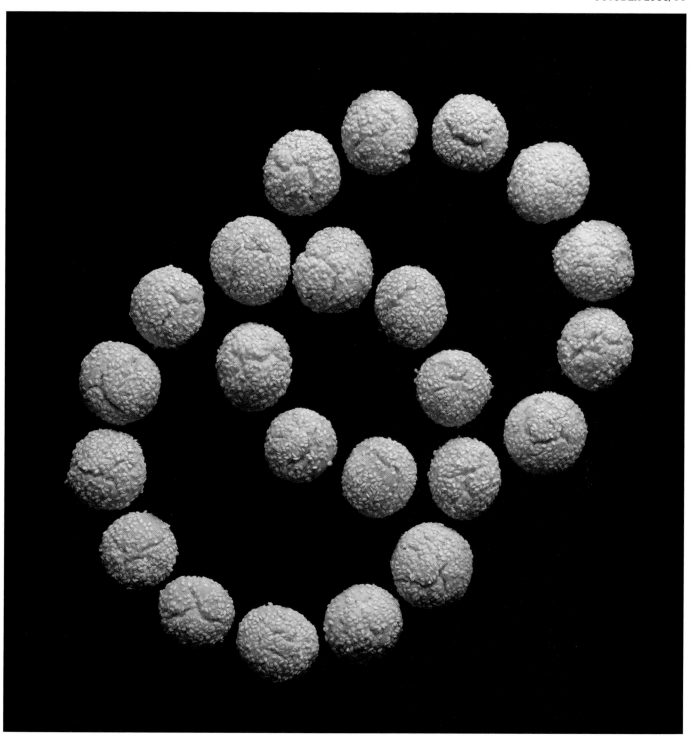

OATMEAL MOLASSES COOKIES

Gourmet never wanted to be a "ladies' magazine," and in the mid-fifties, it did not have a lot of use for cookies; the magazine published only ten recipes for them in 1956. Most were attached to articles on international cooking, but occasionally the magazine's resident chef Louis Diat was moved to provide a recipe or two for readers intent on doing a little cooking for their grandchildren. When Ruth G. Deiches of Los Angeles pleaded for "an oatmeal cookie with a gourmet touch," he cooked up a batch of easy drop cookies filled with raisins and nuts. Did he know how much they would improve with age? They are still great cookies—and they do keep very well.

MAKES ABOUT 12 DOZEN COOKIES

Cream **¼ cup butter** with **1¼ cups sugar**. Add **6 tablespoons molasses** and **2 beaten eggs**, and mix the ingredients thoroughly. Sift together **1¾ cups all-purpose flour** and **1 teaspoon each of soda**, **salt**, and **cinnamon**, and add the dry ingredients to the creamed mixture. Stir in **2 cups quick-cooking rolled oats**, **½ cup chopped nuts**, and **1 cup seedless raisins**. Drop the dough by teaspoons onto a buttered baking sheet, 2 inches apart, and bake the cookies for 10 minutes in a hot oven (400°F).

RECIPE NOTES
1. The butter should be softened before beating (creaming).
2. "Soda" is baking soda.
3. Use walnuts or pecans.

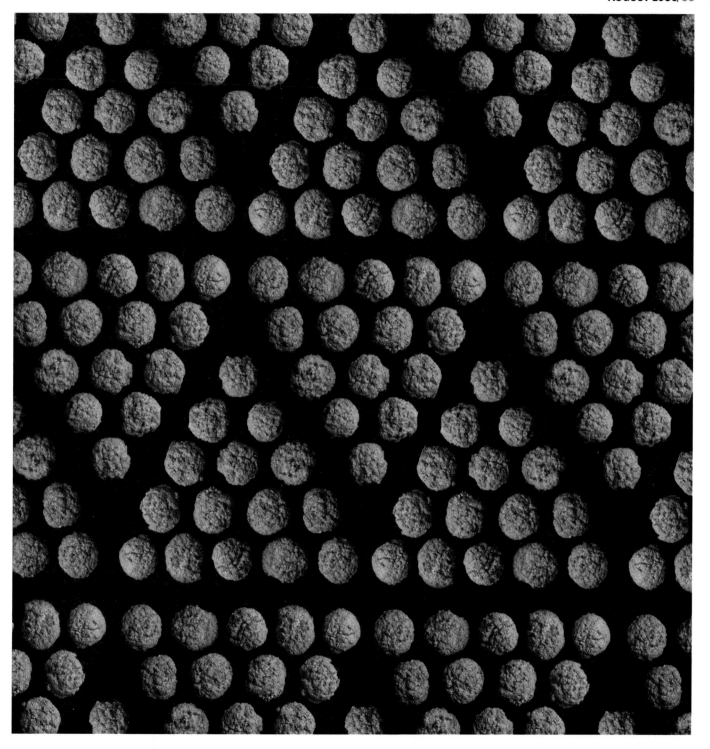

LACE COOKIES

In 1957, *Gourmet* published even fewer cookie recipes than it had the year before; a total of five. Most were dainty treats for grown-ups, such as these little numbers, made with almonds instead of the more usual oatmeal. They appeared as the final flavor in a lavish post-theater menu that began with rich lobster omelets, went on to an exotic salad of romaine lettuce and pineapple, and concluded with a fresh peach compote. Crisp and elegant, with a haunting almond flavor, they make a perfect little tidbit at the end of a meal.

MAKES ABOUT 8 DOZEN COOKIES

Cream **3 tablespoons butter** with **1 cup brown sugar** and beat in **4 tablespoons flour, 1 beaten egg, 1 cup ground almonds, ½ teaspoon almond extract**, and **1 teaspoon vanilla extract**. Drop the dough by teaspoonfuls 3 inches apart on a buttered cooky sheet. Bake the cookies in a moderately hot oven (375°F) for about 8 to 10 minutes, or until they are crisp. Remove the cookies from the pan immediately and cool them on a rack.

RECIPE NOTES
1. The butter should be softened before beating (creaming).
2. Be sure to give the cookies a lot of room on the baking sheet; they will spread.

BRAZIL NUT CRESCENTS

Of the eight cookies *Gourmet* published in 1958, most contained nuts. We were particularly taken with this recipe, because Brazil nuts so rarely figure in the baker's pantry. When you taste these, you'll understand how unfortunate that is. The ground Brazil nuts make a delicately crumbly and irresistibly rich cookie that is fabulous for almost any occasion.

MAKES ABOUT 1½ DOZEN COOKIES

Sift together **1¼ cups sifted flour** and **¼ cup sifted powdered sugar**, and add **1 cup finely ground Brazil nuts**. Cream **½ cup butter**, add the dry ingredients, and knead the dough on a lightly floured board until it is well blended. Form the dough into a roll 2 inches thick and cut it crosswise into ½-inch slices. Shape the slices into crescents, place the crescents on a buttered baking sheet, and bake them in a moderately slow oven (325°F) for 10 minutes, or until they are done. The crescents should not brown.

RECIPE NOTES
1. The butter should be softened before beating (creaming).
2. Use salted butter; the salt brings out the flavor of the nuts.
3. Chill the dough for at least 4 hours before forming it into crescents.
4. Dust the cooled crescents with confectioners' sugar.

GINGERBREAD MEN

This was not the first recipe for gingerbread men that *Gourmet* ran, and it would certainly not be the last. But it is our favorite of a large lot. It came from an article filled with holiday recipes in which time was an essential ingredient. Some required the leisurely attention of the cook during preparation; others could be made ahead and sent out as Christmas greetings. If you decide to send gingerbread men to your friends, this is the one they'll want. As the recipe suggests, time is on their side: the little men improve with age.

MAKES EIGHT 6-INCH COOKIES

Into a bowl, sift **3 cups all-purpose flour**. Add **1½ teaspoons baking powder**, **¼ teaspoon baking soda**, **1 scant tablespoon cinnamon**, **1 teaspoon each of cloves and ginger**, both ground, and **½ teaspoon salt**. Sift the mixture. In another bowl, combine **1 cup brown sugar**, **⅔ cup dark molasses**, **½ cup butter**, **1 beaten egg**, and **¼ teaspoon allspice**, and mix all together well. Stir the brown-sugar mixture into the dry mixture and knead until all the flour has been worked in.
→ Divide the dough and roll it, half at a time, into a sheet ⅓ inch thick. Cut out the gingerbread men with a floured cutter. Transfer the forms to a buttered baking sheet and use pieces of seedless raisins and candied fruits or nuts to make the eyes, nose, and mouth. Bake the gingerbread men in a moderately hot oven (375°F) for 12 minutes, or until they are lightly browned. The gingerbread men may be hung on the Christmas tree.

RECIPE NOTES
1. Use ordinary molasses, not robust.
2. The butter should be softened before mixing.
3. Chill the dough overnight to round out the flavors of the spices and make it easier to roll out.
4. If you want to hang the cookies on the Christmas tree, make a small hole with a chopstick or drinking straw at the top of each cookie before baking them.

1960s

The dramatic growth of consumer jet travel sent Americans off to discover the world in the first half of the decade, and tastes began to change. Cooks were now looking beyond France for recipe inspiration. The turmoil of the later sixties had an impact as well, inspiring American cooks to become more daring. The recipes grew more sophisticated, and unusual ingredients were swirled into the cookies. Suddenly they included pine nuts, candied orange peel, and cottage cheese.

PINE NUT MACAROONS

We tend to think of pine nuts as a foreign ingredient, but in the sixties they were known as "Indian nuts" and considered thoroughly American. The author of this recipe, a transplanted New Yorker who lived in New Mexico, went on an outing with her family to harvest the nuts from the piñon trees, and returned to use them in everything from stuffed escarole to spicy green sauce. In her delightfully chewy cookies, the pliant elasticity of almond paste is set off by the soft, tender richness of the pine nuts. These are identical to the pignoli cookies you'll find in every bakery in every Little Italy in America.

MAKES ABOUT 2 DOZEN COOKIES

Blanch **½ pound almonds** in boiling water and slip off the skins. Pound or grind the almonds to a paste with **2 egg whites**, using a blender, a food chopper, or a mortar and pestle. Work in **1 cup sugar** and flavor the mixture with **2 tablespoons of any desired liqueur**. Shape the dough into small rounds on a buttered baking sheet and brush them with **lightly beaten egg white**. Decorate each macaroon with as many **pine nuts** as it will hold, and set them aside to dry for several hours.
→ Bake the macaroons in a moderate oven (350°F) for about 15 minutes, or until they are delicately colored.

RECIPE NOTES
1. Buy blanched almonds and grind them in a food processor with the egg whites.
2. Make mounds of about 1 tablespoon each, and allow to dry for 3 hours before baking.

BROWN BUTTER COOKIES

A miracle of chemistry: somehow this particular combination of butter, sugar, vanilla, flour, and baking powder creates a textural wonder with a fine sandy character. You've used all these ingredients before, but browning the butter as a first step gives the cookies a complex range of flavors. The recipe comes from a classic sixties ode to the freezer. The author was so taken with the relatively newfangled appliance that she wrote, "There are those among us who feel that the ultimate in strawberry-ness is attained by frozen berries, that their color and flavor is intensified by the freezing process."

MAKES ABOUT 7 DOZEN COOKIES

In a heavy saucepan, melt **1 cup butter** over low heat until it browns. Add **⅔ cup sugar** and **1 tablespoon vanilla sugar** and cool the mixture. Beat in **2⅓ cups flour** and **1 teaspoon baking powder** to make a smooth dough. Roll spoonfuls of the dough into marble-sized balls and put them 1 inch apart on a buttered baking sheet. Press each ball down slightly with the tines of a fork, and top with half a **blanched almond**. Bake the cookies in a moderately slow oven (325°F) for 20 minutes. Remove them from the baking sheet and cool.
→ Serve half of the cookies. Freeze the remainder in a freezer container. To serve the frozen cookies, defrost them at room temperature for 5 to 10 minutes.

RECIPE NOTES
1. To make vanilla sugar, put a vanilla bean into a container of granulated sugar and let it stand for at least 2 days—the longer, the better.
2. The dough is very crumbly, like a shortbread dough, and it must be kneaded to make it come together in a smooth mass; do not be gentle.

COTTAGE CHEESE COOKIES

This is not just the best cookie *Gourmet* published this year: it is the only one. Since the beginning of the decade, Americans were jetting to faraway places much more frequently than they ever had before. This was reflected in the pages of the magazine, which spent more time covering European destinations and less time on nostalgic articles about the past. But although the magazine gave cookies short shrift, when it did come up with a recipe, it was a winner. Cottage cheese in cookies might sound strange, but it is much like ricotta, lending a subtle tang that mellows a sugar cookie into something nuanced and very lovely.

MAKES ABOUT 8 DOZEN COOKIES

Cream together **½ cup softened butter** and **¼ cup cottage cheese**. Blend in thoroughly **1 cup sugar**, **1 teaspoon vanilla**, and **1 egg**. Stir in **2 cups sifted flour** sifted with **½ teaspoon each of baking soda and salt**. Drop the dough from a teaspoon onto a buttered baking sheet, and bake the cookies in a moderately hot oven (375°F) for about 10 minutes, until they are golden brown.

RECIPE NOTE
Use either large- or small-curd cottage cheese (do not drain it).

CURLED WAFERS

Not a single one of the four cookie recipes that appeared in *Gourmet* in 1963 was of American origin. Even though this recipe is from a loving reminiscence about a black Southern cook, it is identical to a Scandinavian krumkake. "How a Scandinavian delicacy found its way to North Georgia I have no idea," wrote the author. But it's easy to understand their appeal; a few eggs, a bit of butter, and some water and flour are magically transformed into crisp, delicate little curls that are the perfect ending to a light lunch.

MAKES ABOUT 2½ DOZEN COOKIES

Beat **3 eggs** with **½ cup sugar** until the mixture is light. Add **½ cup each of cold water and melted and cooled butter**, **½ teaspoon vanilla**, and **1 cup sifted flour**. Stir the mixture until it is smooth. Heat a krumkake iron over low heat and brush it lightly with melted butter. Pour about 1 tablespoon of the batter into the iron; the batter is thin and will spread and cover the surface. Cook the wafers slowly until they are golden on one side, turn them, and cook the other side. Remove each wafer with a fork and roll it to form a cylinder.

RECIPE NOTE
If you don't have a krumkake iron, use an electric pizzelle iron, which allows you to make 2 cookies at a time. Count on 30 to 35 seconds. To order a krumkake iron or an electric pizzelle iron, see Sources (page 154).

FIG COOKIES

Cookies made their triumphant return to the pages of *Gourmet* with a Christmas tribute entitled "Fruitful Cookies." The recipes included tangerinettes, dried apricot cookies, fruitcake cookies, and black walnut strips. But we like these cookies best of all, because they are not only unusual (the dried figs are used more like nuts than fruit), but also gorgeously crumbly and fragrant with the elusive scent of figs.

MAKES ABOUT 4½ DOZEN COOKIES

Cream **1 cup butter**, add **¼ cup sugar**, and beat the mixture until it is fluffy. Stir in **1 cup pecans**, ground, and **1 teaspoon vanilla**. Mix **2 cups sifted flour** with **1 cup ground dried figs** and stir into the creamed mixture. Form the dough into small finger shapes, arrange them on buttered baking sheets, and bake the cookies in a slow oven (300°F) for 25 to 30 minutes. Be careful that they don't brown.

RECIPE NOTES
1. The butter should be softened before beating (creaming).
2. The pecans should be finely ground.
3. Use dried Calimyrna figs; Black Mission figs are too moist and soft. Remove the stems and grind the figs by pulsing in a food processor.
4. Use a scant tablespoon of dough for each cookie and form them into 2½-inch-long logs on the cookie sheet, arranging them about 1½ inches apart. (The batter will spread.)

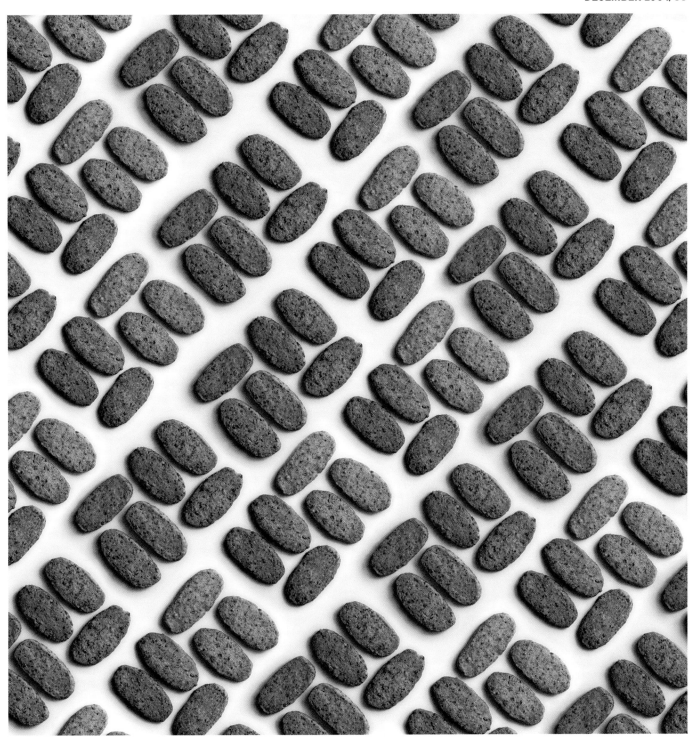

GINGER SUGAR COOKIES

In 1965, *Gourmet*'s idea of a perfect afternoon tea was dear little sandwiches of avocado or watercress, with the crusts cut off, surrounded by a cornucopia of sweets. The menu that these "enticements" came from included an array of thirteen different kinds of cookies and cakes. They're all good, but these are the best: an unforgettable melding of ginger, cinnamon, and cloves that is deepened with molasses. The result is an absolutely classic cookie with rich American roots. This recipe is almost identical to one first published in a Betty Crocker cookbook in the early thirties. No wonder it has had such staying power; the flavor lingers in your mouth long after the last bite has been swallowed.

MAKES ABOUT 11 DOZEN COOKIES

Cream **¾ cup shortening or butter** and gradually beat in **1 cup dark brown sugar**, firmly packed. Stir in **1 egg** and **¼ cup molasses** and blend thoroughly. Sift **2¼ cups sifted flour** with **2 teaspoons baking soda**, **1 teaspoon each of cinnamon and ginger**, **½ teaspoon cloves**, and **¼ teaspoon salt**. Gradually blend the dry ingredients into the creamed mixture and chill the dough for 1 hour.

→ Drop by heaping teaspoons into 1-inch balls and dip the tops in **sugar**. Arrange the balls at least 3 inches apart on a greased baking sheet and sprinkle each cookie with **2 or 3 drops of water**. Bake the cookies in a moderately hot oven (375°F) for about 7 to 8 minutes, or until they are firm.

RECIPE NOTES

1. Either butter or shortening works well. The butter should be softened before beating (creaming).
2. Use ordinary mild molasses, not robust.
3. To form the cookies, scoop out a heaping teaspoon of the dough and dip the top in sugar.
4. Sprinkling the cookies with water gives them their characteristic crackled look.
5. If you take the cookies out of the oven a bit early, when they have just set, they will be soft and slightly chewy. Leave them to bake a little longer, and they'll get crisp.
6. These cookies keep well and are even better on the second day.

APRICOT CHEWS

The world was changing. *Gourmet* ran articles about swinging London; a story about eggplants was called "Purple Passion," written out in swirling, psychedelic type; and one reader letter was entitled "Pecan Cake à Gogo." In the spirit of anything goes, the editors published this much-improved version of a traditional date bar, which was adapted from a recipe from reader Mrs. Hyman Cherenson of Dorchester, Massachusetts. With apricots substituted for the dates, the bars take on an appealingly sweet-and-sour character. The coconut adds a tropical note and fascinating texture. As the editors noted (with a nod to Yogi Berra?), "You have to watch sweets like these. They have a way of disappearing before anyone has had a chance to eat them."

MAKES 3 DOZEN SQUARES

Melt **¾ cup butter**, add **1 cup brown sugar**, **1½ cups each of flour and oatmeal**, and **1 teaspoon baking soda**. Mix the ingredients thoroughly and press half the mixture into a greased baking pan about 9 inches square. In a saucepan, simmer **¾ pound dried apricots** with **1 cup water** and **¾ cup sugar** for 30 minutes, or until the apricots are soft. Add **1 tablespoon apricot liqueur** after the mixture has been cooking for 20 minutes. Spoon the apricots over the crumb mixture in the baking pan, sprinkle them with **¼ cup grated coconut**, if desired, and cover them with the rest of the crumbs. Bake the mixture in a moderate oven (350°F) for 25 to 30 minutes, or until it is golden. Cut the mixture into squares while it is still warm and turn out the chews from the pan when they are cold and set.

RECIPE NOTES
1. For the best flavor and color, use California dried apricots.
2. Use apricot brandy.
3. Puree the apricots in a food processor after cooking.
4. Grease the baking pan with butter, line it with two crisscrossed sheets of foil, and then butter the foil.
5. Make 36 squares by cutting the bars into 6 rows each lengthwise and crosswise.

MANDELBROT (CHOCOLATE ALMOND SLICES)

The cover boasted a cheese soufflé. The menus offered spring luncheons. One included paupiettes of veal on pea puree, mushroom puffs, and praline sabayon. Another was chicken hash Ninette with steamed radishes, as well as meringues with orange cream. The issue also contained recipes for confections known as Marie Josées and Colettes. Seen against a background of such dainty fare, these cookies seem remarkably down to earth. But they are wonderful—crunchy almond cookies with a nutty chocolate heart, a Jewish classic that bears a strong family resemblance to Italian biscotti.

MAKES ABOUT 3½ DOZEN COOKIES

In a bowl, beat **3 eggs** with **¾ cup sugar** until the mixture is thick and light. Stir in **1 tablespoon orange juice** and **1 teaspoon each of grated orange rind and almond extract**. Sift **3 cups sifted flour** with **2 teaspoons baking powder**. Fold half the flour mixture into the egg mixture with **6 tablespoons peanut oil**. Add the remaining flour, plus an **extra ⅓ cup flour**, and beat the mixture for about 30 seconds. Separate one fourth of the dough and stir into it **½ cup split blanched almonds** and **¼ cup cocoa**. Form the dough into a roll about ½ inch in diameter. Add more flour as necessary to form the dough into a roll. → Roll out the remaining dough about ½ inch thick and envelop the cocoa roll with it. Cut the roll in half. Put the rolls side by side on a buttered baking sheet and bake them in a moderately slow oven (325°F) for about 30 minutes. Remove the rolls from the oven and cut them into ½-inch-thick slices while they are still hot. Put the slices on a buttered baking sheet and bake them in a moderately slow oven (325°F) for about 5 minutes.

RECIPE NOTES
1. Use unsweetened cocoa powder.
2. Use grated orange zest (without any of the bitter white pith).
3. For the almonds, use slivered blanched almonds.
4. Roll the chocolate dough into a 22-inch log on a well-floured board. Roll out the remaining dough into a 22-by-3-inch strip on a well-floured board.
5. Arrange the rolls 3 inches apart on the baking sheets.

FLORENTINES

You get a very big bang for remarkably little work in this fabulous pairing of chocolate and orange. These candy-like cookies are mostly fruit, nuts, and chocolate, with just a bit of flour to hold them together. Easy, elegant, and irresistible, they keep very well before they are iced. Once you add the chocolate glaze, be sure to refrigerate them.

MAKES ABOUT 2 DOZEN COOKIES

In a saucepan, mix together **½ cup each of heavy cream and sugar** and **3 tablespoons butter** and bring the mixture to a boil. Remove it from the heat and stir in **1¼ cups finely chopped almonds, ¾ cup finely chopped candied orange peel** (see page 153 and Sources), and **⅓ cup flour**. Drop the batter from a tablespoon into mounds about 3 inches apart on oiled and lightly floured cookie sheets and flatten each cookie with a wet spatula. Bake the cookies in a moderate oven (350°F) for about 10 minutes. Remove them from the oven and let them stand for about 5 minutes. Remove the cookies to a wire rack, let them cool completely, and spread them with chocolate glaze. Chill them.

CHOCOLATE GLAZE
Melt **1 ounce each of unsweetened chocolate and sweet cooking chocolate** over simmering water. Add **2 tablespoons butter** and **1 teaspoon honey** and stir the glaze until the butter is melted. For an easier glaze, use melted bittersweet chocolate.

RECIPE NOTES
1. Use a small offset spatula to spread the dough into thin rounds on the baking sheet.
2. Use 2 ounces semisweet chocolate, melted, for the glaze.

GALETTES DE NOËL (DEEP-FRIED WAFERS)

James Beard was one of *Gourmet*'s first editors, and in the early years, he not only contributed recipes, but also spent months tooling around French vineyards for the magazine. He left after a falling-out with publisher Earle MacAusland in 1950, but in 1969, he made a triumphant return. In the article that included this recipe, he was dreaming of Christmas in Provence and reminiscing about his love for this delicate dessert. His contribution to the traditional recipe was to add a touch of baking powder; he swore that it made the deep-fried wafers even more delicious.

MAKES 15 TO 18 COOKIES

Sift together **4 cups all-purpose flour**, **2 tablespoons sugar**, and **1 teaspoon each of baking powder and salt**. Beat **2 eggs** rather well and beat in approximately ¾ **cup milk**. Combine the egg mixture with the dry ingredients and mix in ½ **stick (¼ cup) butter, melted**. The dough should be easy to handle but not sticky—you may find that you need another spoonful or so of milk.

· Form the dough into about 15 to 18 balls and let them stand, covered with a cloth, for about 25 minutes. Roll them out in circles about 10 inches in diameter. Drop the circles into hot deep fat (370°F) and fry them until they are delicately browned. Remove them carefully and drain them on paper towels. Dredge them with confectioners' sugar and pile them one on top of the other.

· The dough may also be cut into long strips, fried, and dusted with sugar. Sometimes the galettes are dipped into hot honey after being sugared.

RECIPE NOTES
1. Beat the eggs just until they are well combined.
2. Roll out the dough rounds on a lightly floured surface.
3. Fry the galettes, 1 round at a time, in about 8 cups vegetable oil.

1970s

The food processor was introduced in the middle of the seventies, and once-difficult kitchen tasks suddenly became easy. Little wonder, then, that cookie recipes proliferated. But browsing through them, you sense a certain nostalgia creeping in, as if cooks were seeking the comfort of the past as they baked. *Gourmet*'s authors were turning back to their roots, and when they traveled, the cookie recipes that they carried back were intended to re-create the reassuring taste of history.

"SHOE SOLE" COOKIES

"One Christmas," wrote *Gourmet*'s best-loved contributor Lillian Langseth-Christensen, "my wish was for a cocker spaniel; another Christmas, I wanted Mr. Ludwig Bemelmans. But now I am experienced, and I wish for Dallmayr for Christmas." Langseth-Christensen's ode to Munich's beloved food shop makes you long to be there, and the Bavarian recipes make you very hungry. We're particularly fond of these puff-pastry cookies, each one a large and flaky handful. And while these would have been a tour de force in 1970, the advent of frozen puff pastry turned them into a cinch.

MAKES 1 DOZEN COOKIES

Roll out **puff paste** ⅛ inch thick on a heavily sugared pastry board. With an oval cookie cutter, cut the paste into ovals. If a waffle-patterned rolling pin is available, use it to roll out the ovals as large as a shoe sole. Or, roll out the ovals with an ordinary rolling pin and with the back of a knife, make a waffle pattern on each oval. Arrange the ovals, patterned side down, on a baking sheet sprinkled with water and sprinkle them with **confectioners' sugar**. Bake the cookies in a hot oven (425°F) for a few minutes, or until the sugar is browned and glazed. Watch them carefully to make sure they do not burn. With a spatula, remove them to a wire rack to cool.

RECIPE NOTES
1. We use Pepperidge Farm puff paste to make the cookies.
2. Use granulated sugar when you roll out the dough.
3. To make the soles, cut out 5-inch ovals and roll out to 7 inches.
4. The waffle pattern is for decoration only.
5. Bake for 10 to 15 minutes.

SPECULAAS (SAINT NICHOLAS COOKIES)

A former minister of foreign affairs in Holland offended many cooks when he informed the world that the speculaas was Europe's best cookie. That is a matter of opinion, but it is a matter of fact that they are among the oldest cookies on record, for speculaas have been baked in the Netherlands for centuries. They began life as gifts to the gods, left in the fields as offerings to ensure a good harvest. But humans are equally enamored of this cross between a spice cookie and a shortbread because of their comfortingly robust and old-fashioned flavor.

MAKES ABOUT 4 DOZEN COOKIES

Into a bowl, sift together **3 cups flour, 4 teaspoons baking powder, 1 tablespoon cinnamon, 1 teaspoon each of cloves and nutmeg,** and **½ teaspoon each of ground aniseed, salt, and ginger or white pepper**. In a bowl of an electric mixer, beat **2 sticks, or 1 cup, butter, softened,** with **1½ cups firmly packed dark brown sugar** until the mixture is light and fluffy. Stir in **3 tablespoons milk, dark rum, or brandy**. Gradually add the flour mixture, stirring until it is well combined, and form the dough into a ball. Knead the dough on a board sprinkled with about **¼ cup flour** and roll it out into a rectangle ¼ inch thick. With a sharp knife or cutter, cut the dough into rectangles 2½ inches by 1½ inches. Put the rectangles on a buttered cookie sheet, decorate them with **blanched almonds**, halved or slivered, and brush them with **lightly beaten egg white**. Bake the cookies in a moderately hot oven (375°F) for 12 to 15 minutes, or until they are browned and firm.

RECIPE NOTE
Gently push the nuts into the dough before brushing the cookies with egg white.

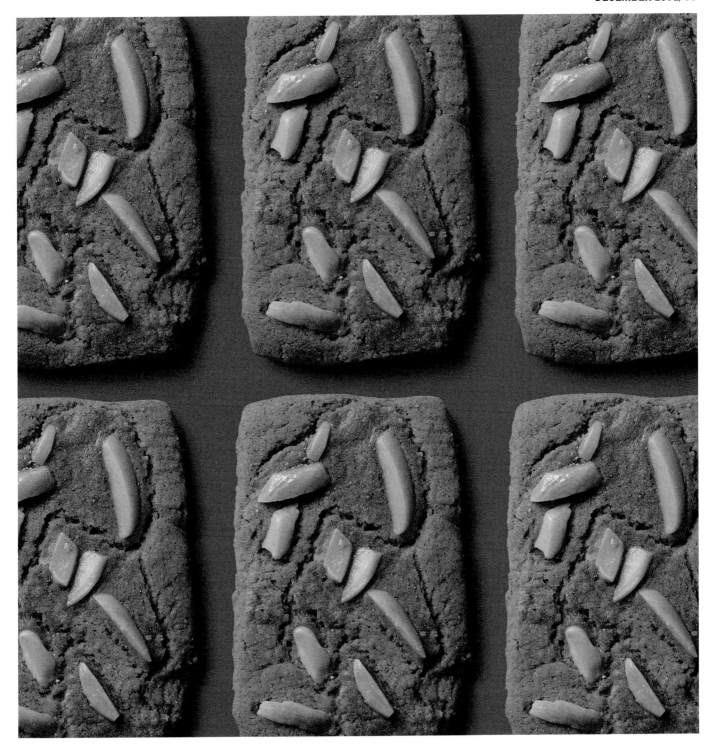

DUTCH CARAMEL CASHEW COOKIES

This recipe was collected by the cookbook author Lou Seibert Pappas, who went around the world while in the throes of a deep praline addiction. Her most wonderful find was this irresistible confection, which is sweet, salty, and crunchy. You begin by making candy. Then you chop it up and fold most of it into cookie dough, leaving a bit to scatter on top. The result is something truly spectacular. Streaked with nuts, the cookies crunch and crackle with every bite.

MAKES ABOUT 1½ DOZEN COOKIES

MAKE CASHEW PRALINE: In a heavy skillet, cook **½ cup sugar** with **2 tablespoons water** and a **pinch of cream of tartar** over moderately high heat, washing down any undissolved sugar that clings to the sides of the skillet with a brush dipped in cold water, until the mixture is a light caramel. Stir in quickly **½ cup finely chopped roasted salted cashews**. Pour the praline onto a buttered piece of foil and, with a buttered spatula, spread it into a thin sheet. Let it cool until it hardens, and chop it coarsely.

→ In a bowl, beat **1 stick (½ cup) butter** with **⅓ cup sugar** until it is creamy. Beat in **1 egg yolk** and **½ teaspoon vanilla**. Stir in **1 cup flour** and two thirds of the chopped praline and form the mixture into a dough. Roll the dough into logs 2½ inches long and ¾ inch wide and put them about 2 inches apart on a lightly buttered cookie sheet. Sprinkle the logs with the remaining praline and bake them in a moderate oven (350°F) for 12 to 15 minutes, or until they are lightly browned. Let the cookies cool on the sheet for about 1 minute and with a spatula remove them to a rack to cool completely.

RECIPE NOTE
The butter should be softened before beating.

CRESCENT CHEESE COOKIES

Gourmet was no longer produced in the penthouse at the Plaza, and "Gourmet's Chef" had been replaced with a serious test kitchen. So when a reader wrote in requesting a recipe for something her mother used to make—"a delicious cookie made with pot cheese and filled with jam"—*Gourmet*'s cooks responded with these rich little pastries that are like the most delicate, flaky rugelach imaginable.

MAKES ABOUT 2½ DOZEN COOKIES

Force enough **pot cheese** through a sieve into a dish to measure **1 cup.** In a bowl, cream **2 sticks, or 1 cup, butter, softened**, until it is smooth, stir in the sieved cheese, **2 tablespoons sour cream**, and **¼ teaspoon vanilla**, and combine the mixture well. Into another bowl, sift together **2 cups flour** and **¼ teaspoon salt**, and gradually blend the flour mixture into the cheese mixture. Wrap the dough in wax paper and chill it for at least 3 hours.
→ Roll one fourth of the dough out very thinly on a lightly floured surface and chill the remaining dough until it is to be used. Cut the dough
into 3-inch squares and put about **½ teaspoon jam or preserves** in the center of each. Fold the squares tightly into triangles and roll them into crescents, starting at the wide end. Arrange the crescents on a baking sheet, brush them lightly with milk, and bake them in a preheated hot oven (400°F) for 15 to 20 minutes, or until they are golden. Transfer the cookies to a wire rack and dust them with sifted confectioners' sugar. Continue making cookies in the same manner until all the dough is used.

RECIPE NOTES
1. Pot cheese is a very dry version of low-fat cottage cheese; if you can't find it, use farmer cheese. It takes about 6 ounces sieved cheese to make 1 cup.
2. Do not roll the dough too thin—⅛ inch is perfect.
3. Use your fingers to roll the triangles into crescents, curving up on the narrow corners.

KOURAMBIEDES (GREEK BUTTER COOKIES)

Leon Lianides was the owner of the Coach House Restaurant in Greenwich Village, where he served predominantly Southern food. But he was also fiercely proud of his Greek origins, and when he wrote about his native land, he did so with enormous love. His recipes, like this one, are utterly simple and completely authentic. These buttery bites have the tenderness of ground almonds kissed with a faint touch of orange. The cloves are meant to be removed before eating.

MAKES ABOUT 4 DOZEN COOKIES

In the bowl of an electric mixer, cream **4 sticks, or 2 cups, butter, softened**, at low speed for 1 hour, or until it is almost white. Add **¼ cup confectioners' sugar**, sifted, 1 tablespoon at a time, **1 egg yolk**, and **1 tablespoon orange-flavored liqueur or brandy**, and blend in **4½ cups flour** and **½ cup finely ground blanched almonds,** ½ cup at a time, to form a soft dough. (If the dough seems sticky, chill it, wrapped in wax paper, for 1 hour.) Form the dough into 1½-inch balls and stud each ball with **1 clove**. Put the balls on baking sheets and bake them in a preheated moderate oven (350°F) for 15 minutes, or until they are pale golden. Transfer the cookies to a rack, let them cool for 2 minutes, and dredge them in sifted confectioners' sugar.

RECIPE NOTE
A stand mixer will cream the butter in about 8 minutes.

ALMOND BOLAS (PORTUGUESE ALMOND COOKIES)

In April 1975, *Gourmet* introduced "the phenomenal food processor" to its readers, enthusing that it "speedily handles so many time-consuming culinary exercises that it brings epicurean feats frequently into the realm of everyday fare." It certainly turns this unusual cookie into a fairly easy treat. What makes the recipe so special—and characterizes it as Portuguese—is the beaten egg at the heart of each cookie, which lends it an appealingly rich character.

MAKES ABOUT 4 DOZEN COOKIES

In a bowl, combine **3 cups ground blanched almonds** and **1½ cups each of dry bread crumbs and sugar**. Fold in **3 egg whites**, beaten until they hold stiff peaks, and **1½ teaspoons almond extract**. Form tablespoons of the mixture into balls and put the balls on buttered baking sheets. In a small bowl, beat **3 egg yolks** with **1 whole egg**. Make an indentation in each ball and fill the hollows with beaten egg. Cap each egg-filled ball with a **lightly toasted blanched almond** and bake the cookies in a preheated moderate oven (350°F) for 15 minutes, or until they are golden.

RECIPE NOTES
1. Buy 1 pound of blanched almonds and grind them in batches in a food processor.
2. If you are using store-bought bread crumbs, buy a new package for this recipe; they tend to go stale easily.
3. Use ½ teaspoon beaten egg for each cookie.

LEMON THINS

A sign that things were changing: for the first time since the end of World War II, *Gourmet* introduced cookies that were not part of an article about a country, attached to a menu, or honoring a holiday. In an article simply entitled "Butter Cookies," the magazine gave "these beguiling dainties" their due. Each of the recipes was excellent, but we're particularly partial to these, which capture the bright sourness of lemons, so that each unassuming bite packs a punch of citrus flavor.

MAKES ABOUT 4 DOZEN COOKIES

In a bowl, beat **2 eggs** with **⅔ cup sugar** and **½ teaspoon vanilla** for 3 to 4 minutes, or until the mixture forms a ribbon when the beater is lifted, and add **2 teaspoons grated lemon rind**. In a bowl, beat **¾ stick (6 tablespoons) butter, softened**, until it is light and fluffy and add it to the egg mixture alternately with **⅔ cup flour**. Drop the batter by teaspoons 2½ inches apart on buttered baking sheets, flatten the mounds into 2-inch rounds with a spoon dipped in water, and bake the cookies in a preheated hot oven (400°F) for 5 minutes, or until the edges are browned. Let the cookies cool on the sheets for 1 minute, transfer them with a spatula to a rack, and let them cool completely.

RECIPE NOTES
1. Use an electric mixer to beat the eggs with the sugar, and don't be surprised if it takes more than 4 minutes to ribbon the mixture.
2. Use grated lemon zest (without any of the bitter white pith).

IRISH COFFEE CRUNCHIES

"This month," wrote the editors as they introduced the August issue, "we escape the familiar." The getaways included a voyage to Western Samoa, a fishing trip to the Ozarks, and an opportunity to "revel among the home-baked cakes and confections of Irish Protestant fêtes." At one of those celebrations in County Cork, the crime novelist Michael Kenyon encountered what was, for him, an unfamiliar cookie, made with Irish whiskey, coffee, and heavy cream. It's little wonder that he was so taken with this cookie: like so many of his characters, its rough exterior hides a heart that is both sweet and smooth.

MAKES ABOUT 1½ DOZEN COOKIES

In a bowl, beat **1 stick (½ cup) butter, softened**, with **¼ cup sugar** until the mixture is fluffy. Beat in **2 teaspoons each of Irish whiskey and strong coffee** and **1 teaspoon heavy cream**. Add **2 cups quick-cooking oats** and **1 cup flour** sifted with **1 teaspoon double-acting baking powder** and combine the mixture to form a dough. Roll out the dough ⅛ inch thick on a floured surface and, with a 2¼-inch cutter, cut out rounds. Bake the rounds on a buttered baking sheet in a preheated moderate oven (350°F) for 15 minutes, or until they are lightly colored. Transfer the rounds to a rack and let them cool.
→ In a small bowl, combine **2 teaspoons each of Irish whiskey and strong coffee** and **1 teaspoon heavy cream**. In a bowl combine **½ cup confectioners' sugar**, sifted, and the coffee mixture, stir in **3 teaspoons boiling water**, a little at a time, and beat the icing, adding a few drops more water if necessary, until it is smooth and of spreading consistency. Spread half the rounds thinly with the icing, and top them with the remaining rounds. Transfer the cookies to a rack and let the icing set.

RECIPE NOTE
This is a very dry dough, so you have to knead it to get it to come together; do not be gentle.

BIZCOCHITOS (ANISE COOKIES)

Americans were just beginning to become interested, once again, in their own regional cookies. A piece about the joys of Santa Fe mentioned that New Mexico boasted the first state cookie in the U.S., the bizcochito. It's the most tender creation you can imagine, with an extraordinarily flaky texture and an unusual flavor that comes from the combination of fresh lard, whole wheat flour, and ground anise seed. Think ahead: the cookies are wonderful when they come out of the oven, but they definitely improve with age.

MAKES ABOUT 3 DOZEN COOKIES

In a large bowl, cream together **1 cup lard** and **¾ cup sugar** until the mixture is light and fluffy and beat in **1 egg**, lightly beaten, and **1½ teaspoons aniseed**. In a bowl, sift together **1½ cups each of whole wheat flour and all-purpose flour**, **1½ teaspoons double-acting baking powder**, and **1 teaspoon salt** and stir the mixture into the lard mixture with **¼ cup brandy or water** until the dough is smooth. Roll out pieces of the dough ⅛ inch thick on a floured surface and, with a 3-inch decorative cutter, cut out cookies. Put the cookies ½ inch apart on baking sheets, sprinkle them generously with **½ cup sugar mixed** with **½ teaspoon cinnamon**, and bake them in a preheated moderate oven (350°F) for 12 to 15 minutes, or until they are golden. Transfer the cookies to racks to cool, and store them in an airtight container for 5 days before serving.

RECIPE NOTES
1. The lard, which can be found in supermarkets with the vegetable shortening, should be at room temperature.
2. Use ground anise.

LINZER BARS

In New York City, Le Cirque had a new chef who was charging outrageous prices for dinner: appetizers cost $2.50! In California, *Gourmet*'s correspondent confessed that she had a weakness for dim sum, green-corn tamales, cumin-scented Moroccan salads, and chile-hot Hunanese food. Cookbook author Nina Simonds had begun a two-year-long series on Chinese cooking. Amid all this, the magazine seemed almost embarrassed to offer its readers a column on bar cookies. Linzer cookies come in many different shapes, and we like them all, but these bars stand out because they combine the appeal of a cookie with the ease of a tart. Simply pat the dough into the pan, spread with jelly, and top with a lattice crust, then cut into squares after baking.

MAKES 32 BARS

In a large bowl, cream together **1 stick (½ cup) butter, softened, ½ cup firmly packed light brown sugar,** and **¼ cup white sugar** until the mixture is light and fluffy and stir in **⅔ cup almonds**, lightly toasted and ground, and **1 egg**, lightly beaten. Into a bowl, sift together **1½ cups flour, ¾ teaspoon double-acting baking powder, ½ teaspoon cinnamon**, and **¼ teaspoon salt**, stir the mixture into the almond mixture, and combine the dough well. Press two thirds of the dough into an 8-inch-square baking pan and, with a spatula, spread **¾ cup raspberry jam** combined with **1 teaspoon grated lemon rind** over it. Roll out the remaining dough ⅛ inch thick between sheets of wax paper and chill it for 15 minutes, or until it is firm. Peel off the top sheet of paper, cut the dough into ½-inch strips, and arrange the strips in a lattice pattern over the jam. Bake the dessert in a preheated moderately hot oven (375°F) for 20 to 30 minutes, or until it is golden brown. Sift confectioners' sugar evenly over the top of the dessert, let the dessert cool, and with a serrated knife cut it into 2-by-1-inch bars.

RECIPE NOTES
1. Use grated lemon zest (without any of the bitter white pith).
2. Butter the baking pan, line it with two crisscrossed sheets of foil, and butter the foil.

1980s

"We are a country in which, gastronomically, menus and even individual dishes more and more frequently are a surprising, delectable, global mixture, the 'foreign' cozying up to, even infiltrating, the American," wrote the author and bon vivant Leo Lerman in a 1984 roundup of cookbooks. You can't help noticing this trend when tracking the influences in the cookie recipes of the eighties.

BOURBON BALLS

The 1980s were the beginning of the cookie years at *Gourmet*: in the recipe index for 1980, cookie recipes outnumber those for lobster, shrimp, or pastry. When the food editors cooked up an elegant midnight buffet of a crab roulade, pheasant, mushrooms smitane, and wild rice waffles, they ended the meal with dense, moist, and very easy no-bake cookies. A child could make them, but these bourbon balls are definitely not for children.

MAKES ABOUT 3 DOZEN BALLS

In a small bowl, let **½ cup chopped raisins** macerate in **¼ cup bourbon** for 15 minutes. In a large bowl, combine well **2 cups chocolate wafer crumbs, ½ cup each of firmly packed dark brown sugar and finely chopped pecans**, the raisin mixture, **¼ cup unsulfured molasses, ½ teaspoon each of cinnamon and ground ginger**, and **¼ teaspoon ground cloves**. Form the mixture into 1-inch balls and roll the balls in **finely chopped pecans**. Store the bourbon balls in an airtight container in a cool dark place for at least 1 week before serving.

RECIPE NOTES
1. You'll need 4½ ounces chocolate wafer cookies (Famous is one brand) to make 2 cups of crumbs.
2. Use ordinary molasses, not robust.

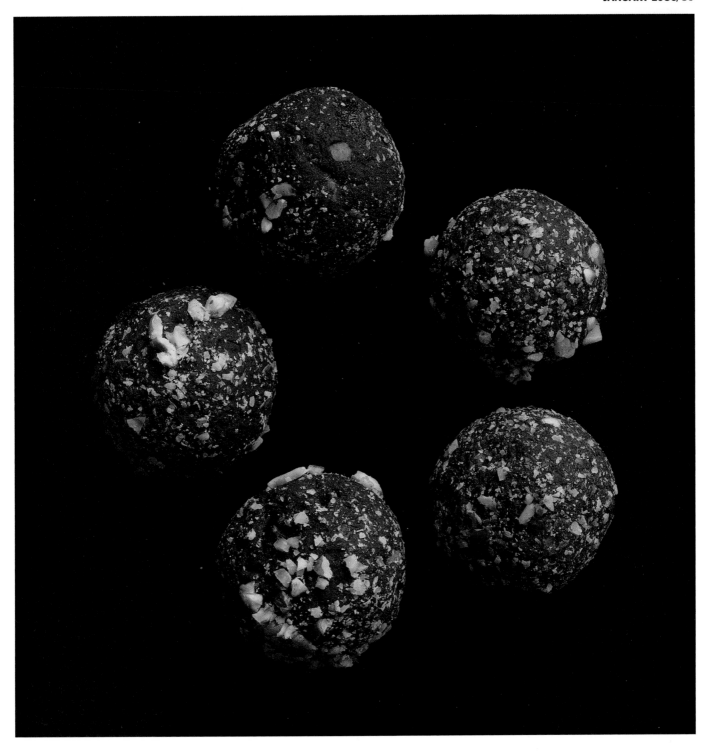

CLOUDT'S PECAN TREATS

Gourmet was beginning to honor a new geography of cooking, as articles about American food appeared more frequently in its pages. In the past, most of the big travel features had taken readers to faraway places, but in this issue, the trip was to Atlanta, which was treated as an exotic location. The writer painted an appealing picture of Cloudt's grocery store, a local institution that was also a lunch or dinner spot. A piano player made soft music while diners wandered past the fruits and vegetables to select meals from dishes laid on tables in the aisles. Of the many Southern recipes she brought back from her sojourn—oysters en brochette with bacon, chocolate walnut pie—the most appealing was this one. The enormously rich and nutty squares will remind you of a French nut tart, but they require a fraction of the effort.

MAKES 35 BARS

In a bowl, cream together **1½ sticks (¾ cup) unsalted butter, softened, ¾ cup granulated sugar,** and **¾ teaspoon salt** until the mixture is light and fluffy and beat in **1 large egg plus 2 tablespoons lightly beaten egg**. Add **2¾ cups all-purpose flour** and stir the mixture until it is just blended. Press the mixture evenly into a 15½-by-10½-inch jelly-roll pan, bake it in the middle of a preheated moderately hot oven (375°F) for 15 to 20 minutes, or until it is golden, and let it cool in the pan on a rack.

→ In a large heavy saucepan, combine **1⅓ cups firmly packed light brown sugar, 1 stick (½ cup) unsalted butter,** cut into pieces, **½ cup honey,** and **¼ cup half-and-half** and bring the mixture to a boil over moderate heat, stirring. Stir in **14 ounces (about 3¾ cups) pecans, chopped,** and let the mixture cool. Spread the pecan mixture evenly over the shortbread base and bake the dessert in the middle of a preheated moderately hot oven (375°F) for 15 minutes, or until the top is bubbly. Let the dessert cool in the pan on a rack, and cut it into pieces about 2 inches square.

CHOCOLATE MERINGUE BISCUITS

Gourmet had always assumed that its readers were accomplished cooks, printing recipes that were written in a conversational manner, as if one cook was simply telling them to another in a kind of verbal shorthand. When the magazine changed the recipe format in 1982, it was a sign of how much things had evolved in America. No longer able to count on the readers' experience, *Gourmet* tried to make the recipe more accessible by separating the ingredients from the directions.

You actually need very few ingredients for these delicate cloud-light almond meringues, which are a play on pure texture. They weigh almost nothing, but when you put one of them into your mouth, it crunches audibly. Then the cookie slowly begins to dissolve, leaving the chocolate to linger in your mouth along with the faintest memory of meringue.

MAKES ABOUT 4 DOZEN MERINGUES

3 large egg whites, at room temperature, **¼ teaspoon cream of tartar**, **⅓ cup sugar**, **½ teaspoon almond extract**, **½ cup ground blanched almonds**, **4 ounces semisweet chocolate**

In a bowl with an electric mixer, beat the egg whites at moderate speed until they are foamy, add the cream of tartar, and beat the whites until they hold soft peaks. Add the sugar, a little at a time, and the almond extract, beating, then beat the meringue until it holds very stiff peaks, and fold in the almonds, a little at a time.
→ Cover 2 baking sheets with parchment paper and attach the paper by putting a dab of the meringue on the underside of each corner. Drop rounded teaspoons of the meringue 2 inches apart on the baking sheets, bake the meringues in the lower third of a preheated very slow oven (200°F) for 45 to 50 minutes, or until they are firm and dry, and loosen them from the paper with the tip of a small knife. (The meringues may be prepared up to this point and stored in an airtight container for up to 2 weeks.) Spread a thin layer of the chocolate, melted and cooled, on the bottom of each meringue and attach 2 meringues bottom to bottom. Transfer the meringues to a rack set in a cool, dry place and let them stand for 1 hour, or until the chocolate is hard.

RECIPE NOTES
1. Use a piping bag with a plain ½-inch tip to give the cookies their iconic shape.
2. Do not allow the filling to cool before sandwiching the cookies together.

SPRITZ
(NORWEGIAN BUTTER COOKIES)

"My pioneer mother," wrote Carrie Young, who brought a touch of *Little House on the Prairie* to *Gourmet*, "was fond of saying that anyone could be a fine cook if unlimited ingredients were available. To prepare delicious food with what one had on hand was the real challenge." Little wonder, then, that these simple cookies were her mother's favorite. They have no frills, but they are rich, very buttery, and utterly classic.

MAKES ABOUT 6 DOZEN COOKIES

3 sticks (1½ cups) unsalted butter, softened, **1 cup sugar**, **1½ teaspoons vanilla**, **½ teaspoon almond extract**, **1 large egg**, beaten lightly, **4 cups all-purpose flour** sifted with **½ teaspoon double-acting baking powder** and **½ teaspoon salt**

In a large bowl, cream the butter, beat in the sugar, a little at a time, the vanilla, and the almond extract, and beat the mixture until it is light and fluffy. Add the egg and combine the mixture well. Add the flour mixture and combine the dough well. Form the dough into walnut-size balls and arrange the balls 3 inches apart on ungreased baking sheets. Using a fork, flatten the balls to form cookies ⅓ to ½ inch thick, making a crosshatch design. Bake the cookies in a preheated moderate oven (350°F) for 10 to 15 minutes, or until they are golden around the edges, and transfer them with a spatula to racks to cool. Store the cookies in airtight containers.

RECIPE NOTE
You can make these with a cookie press, but we like them just as much when they are baked in rounds, the way Young's mother did, or pipe them into little S's using a pastry bag fitted with a ½-inch star tip.

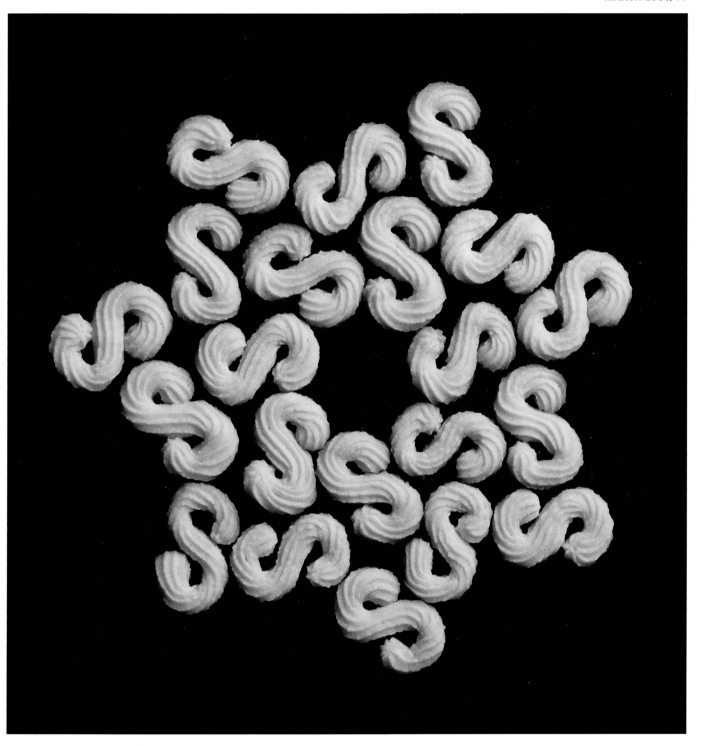

SOUVAROFFS (BUTTER COOKIES WITH JAM)

The magazine's recipe format changed once again in 1984. Now the ingredients were lined up as a kind of shopping list that you could check before you began to cook. The directions changed too, into the terse language that we now consider de rigueur for recipes. This recipe belonged to *Gourmet* contributor Lillian Langseth-Christensen. Known as Liesl, she was an extraordinary writer and designer as well as a talented baker. She lived in a hunting lodge outside Vienna, where she developed recipes using American ingredients that she bought at the PX on a nearby U.S. military base. We have hundreds of her recipes, but we particularly like these buttery treats filled with apricot or strawberry jam. A little rum in the dough sets off its tangy sweetness.

MAKES ABOUT 3½ DOZEN SANDWICH COOKIES

FOR THE DOUGH
1¾ cups all-purpose flour
½ cup confectioners' sugar
1½ sticks (¾ cup) cold unsalted butter, cut into bits
1 large egg yolk, beaten lightly
½ teaspoon light rum or vanilla

⅔ cup jam such as apricot or strawberry, heated and strained

MAKE THE DOUGH: Into a bowl, sift together the flour and the sugar, add the butter, and blend the mixture until it resembles meal. Add the egg yolk, the rum, and 2 tablespoons ice water, toss the mixture until it is combined, and form the dough into a ball. Knead the dough lightly with the heel of the hand against a smooth surface for a few seconds to distribute the fat evenly, and re-form it into a ball. Dust the dough with flour and chill it, wrapped in wax paper, for 30 minutes.

→ Halve the dough, roll out half of it ⅛ inch thick on a floured surface, and cut it into rounds with a 1½-inch fluted cutter. Gather the scraps together, reroll them, and cut out more rounds. Roll out the remaining half of the dough ⅛ inch thick and cut out more rounds in the same manner. Cut out the center of half the rounds with a ½-inch plain round cutter to form rings. Bake the rounds and rings in batches on greased baking sheets in the middle of a preheated 325°F oven for 12 minutes, or until the edges are faintly golden. Transfer the cookies to a rack and let them cool. Sandwich the cookies together with the jam.

RECIPE NOTES
1. Roll out the dough between sheets of parchment or wax paper.
2. For cleaner edges, chill or freeze the dough before and after cutting the rounds.
3. After sandwiching the cookies, use extra jam to top off the centers.

PECAN TASSIES

Didn't get enough pecan pie at Thanksgiving? A tassie is a miniature tart, and when it is as intensely sweet and superbly rich as this, it provides the perfect amount of pie. Each tassie offers a few indulgent bites of butter-drenched nuts enfolded in a cream cheese pastry. Not only are they adorable, they look splendid sitting on a tray.

MAKES 2 DOZEN CONFECTIONS

- 1 stick (½ cup) plus 1 tablespoon unsalted butter, softened slightly
- 3 ounces cream cheese, softened slightly
- 1 cup all-purpose flour
- 1 large egg
- ¾ cup firmly packed light brown sugar
- ½ cup chopped pecans
- ⅛ teaspoon vanilla

In a bowl, combine 1 stick of the butter and the cream cheese, stir in the flour, and form the dough into a ball. Divide the dough into 24 pieces and press the pieces into the bottom and up the sides of 24 small (2-tablespoon) muffin tins. In a small bowl, beat the egg lightly with the brown sugar and stir in the pecans, the remaining 1 tablespoon butter, the vanilla, and a pinch of salt. Divide the filling among the pastry-lined tins, bake the tassies in a preheated 350°F oven for 25 minutes, or until the filling is puffed slightly and the pastry is golden, and let them cool on a rack.

PASTELITOS DE BODA (BRIDE'S COOKIES)

In an article on Mexican desserts, the culinary writer and cookbook author Elisabeth Lambert Ortiz noted that desserts were not an important part of the ancient Mexican kitchen. The Aztecs and Maya had no wheat flour, milk, cream, butter, sugar, or chicken eggs. It was not until the colonial era that dessert as we know it came to Mexico, thanks to the nuns who arrived after the Spanish conquest. So it is little wonder that these cookies so closely resemble classic European nut cookies. By substituting native pecans for the more traditional almonds or hazelnuts, however, the good sisters invented a richer, more tender cookie.

MAKES ABOUT 2 DOZEN COOKIES

- 2 cups all-purpose flour
- ½ cup confectioners' sugar, sifted, plus additional for dusting the cookies
- 1 cup pecans, ground fine in batches in a spice grinder
- 1 teaspoon vanilla
- 2 sticks (1 cup) unsalted butter, softened

Into a bowl, sift together the flour, ½ cup of the confectioners' sugar, the pecans, and a pinch of salt, stir in the vanilla, and blend in the butter until the mixture is combined well. Scoop out rounded tablespoons of the mixture, form them into ¼-inch-thick rounds, and bake the rounds on baking sheets in the middle of a preheated 350°F oven for 10 to 12 minutes, or until they are golden around the edges. Transfer the cookies to racks, let them cool slightly, and sift the additional confectioners' sugar over them.

RECIPE NOTES
1. Use a food processor to grind the pecans.
2. You can flatten the cookies as you place them on the baking sheets.

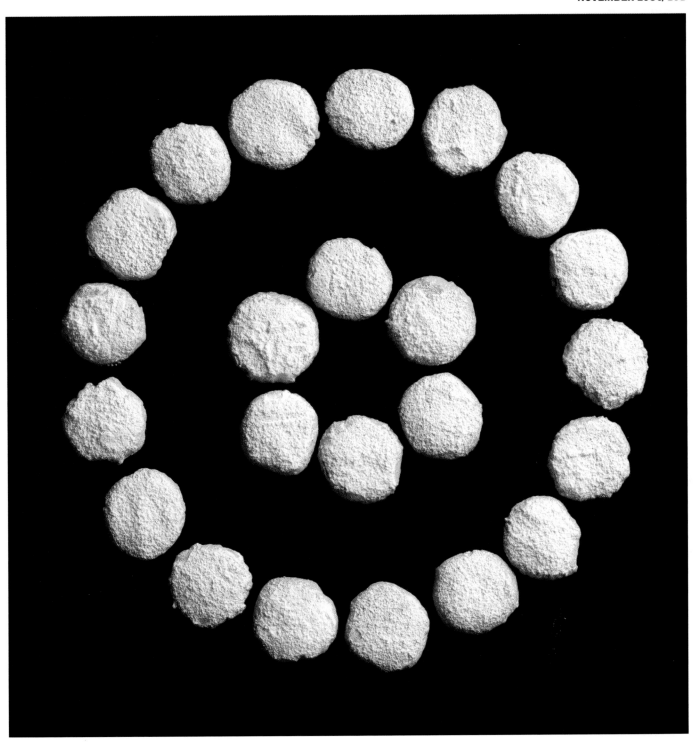

MOCHA TOFFEE BARS

The stock market had just crashed, and *Gourmet* tried to cheer up its readers with visions of a prosperous and patriotic holiday season. The food writer Laurie Colwin dreamed of gingerbread, the cookbook author Barbara Kafka offered recipes for great American cakes, and the Christmas dinner menu featured peppery lobster soup, crown roast of smoked pork with wild rice, and butternut squash with ginger butter. If that weren't enough, you could opt for this decadent combination of buttery toffee and chocolate. As much candy as cookie, the bars are embellished with salty roasted cashews that underline their sweetness.

MAKES 4 DOZEN BARS

- 2 sticks (1 cup) unsalted butter, softened
- 1 cup firmly packed brown sugar
- 1 large egg yolk
- 1½ teaspoons vanilla
- 3 tablespoons instant espresso powder, dissolved in 2 tablespoons boiling water
- ½ teaspoon salt
- 2 cups all-purpose flour
- 8 ounces semisweet chocolate
- ¾ cup salted roasted cashews, chopped

In a bowl with an electric mixer, cream the butter, add the brown sugar, and beat the mixture until it is light and fluffy. Beat in the yolk, add the vanilla and the espresso mixture, a little at a time, beating, and beat the mixture until it is combined well. Add the salt and the flour, beating, and beat the mixture until is combined well. Spread the batter evenly in a jelly-roll pan, 15½ by 10½ by 1 inch, and bake it in the middle of a preheated 350°F oven for 15 to 20 minutes, or until it pulls away slightly from the edge of the pan.
→ Spread the chocolate, melted, evenly over the baked layer and sprinkle the cashews over it. Let the mixture cool in the pan on a rack, cut it into 48 bars, and chill it for 15 to 20 minutes, or until the chocolate is firm.

RECIPE NOTES
1. To offset the sweetness of these bars, we recommend substituting bittersweet chocolate for the semisweet.
2. Butter the pan, line it with two crisscrossed sheets of foil, and butter the foil.

PISTACHIO TUILES

What petits fours, those small icing-covered confections, were to the well-heeled in the 1950s, tuiles were to the 1980s; they garnished every dessert plate in the land. They appeared in *Gourmet* at the end of a trendy summer luncheon menu of mushroom salad, Thai-style steak and green bean salad with spicy mint dressing, and coconut parfaits. Thin and crisp as potato chips, the slim little cookies are studded with pistachios, which give them their delicate color and their elegantly exotic air.

MAKES ABOUT 1 DOZEN COOKIES

- 2 tablespoons unsalted butter, softened
- ¼ cup confectioners' sugar
- ¼ teaspoon almond extract
- 1 large egg white, at room temperature
- 2 tablespoons all-purpose flour
- ¼ cup shelled natural pistachio nuts, blanched and oven-dried and chopped

In a bowl, cream the butter, add the sugar, and beat the mixture until it is light and fluffy. Add the almond extract, the egg white, and a pinch of salt, and beat the mixture for 5 to 10 seconds, or until it is smooth but not frothy. Sift the flour over the mixture and fold it in with the pistachios. (The batter will be thin.) Spoon rounded teaspoons of the batter 3 inches apart onto buttered baking sheets and, with a fork dipped in cold water, spread them to form 2-inch rounds. Bake the cookies in batches in the middle of a preheated 350°F oven for 6 to 9 minutes, or until the edges are golden brown. Transfer the cookies with a metal spatula to a rolling pin and curve them around the pin. (If the cookies become too firm to remove from the baking sheet, return them to the oven for a few seconds to soften.) Let the cookies cool on the rolling pin. The cookies may be made 1 day in advance and kept in an airtight container.

RECIPE NOTES
1. The pistachios do not need to be blanched; simply rub off any loose skins.
2. To form the cookies, drop level tablespoons of batter onto the baking sheets and spread into a thin 3-inch round with an offset spatula.

CORNETTI (ALMOND COOKIES)

By 1989 America was beginning its long love affair with Italian food. In the "Gastronomie sans Argent" column, the editors proffered recipes for winter pasta sauces. The magazine's West Coast critic reveled in bruschetta, spiedini, and risotto at the two-year-old restaurant Olivetto. And one reader wrote in to request a recipe for a cookie she had tasted at the Italian Bakery in Victoria, British Columbia.

Try it, and you'll understand why. The cookie, from an old family recipe from Turin, is made with ground almonds and cornmeal, which lend it an unusual and appealing gravelly texture. The aroma of the finely chopped candied orange peel permeates the dough so that in your first bite, you simultaneously taste fruit, sugar, and nuts.

MAKES 2 DOZEN COOKIES

2⅓ cups finely ground blanched almonds, plus 1 cup coarsely chopped blanched almonds
1 cup white cornmeal (not stone-ground)
1 cup all-purpose flour
2 cups granulated sugar
1 cup finely chopped candied orange peel
5 large egg whites
1 teaspoon vanilla
1¼ cups confectioners' sugar

In a bowl with an electric mixer, beat together the ground almonds, the cornmeal, the flour, the granulated sugar, the rind, the whites, and the vanilla until the mixture forms a dough, and divide the dough into 3 pieces. Sprinkle 1 cup of the confectioners' sugar onto a clean work surface, on the surface roll the dough into 10-inch-long logs, and chill the logs, uncovered, on a jelly-roll pan overnight.

→ Cut each log crosswise into 8 pieces and, with moistened hands, form each piece into a 3-inch-long oval with tapered ends. Dip the ovals in the chopped almonds, sprinkle them with the remaining ¼ cup confectioners' sugar, and form them into crescent shapes, arranging them 1 inch apart on 2 buttered baking sheets.
→ Let the cookies dry at room temperature for 2 hours, and bake them in the upper third of a preheated 450°F oven for 7 to 8 minutes, or until they are pale golden. Transfer the cookies with a spatula to racks and let them cool.

RECIPE NOTES
1. You'll need 13 ounces blanched almonds to make 2⅓ cups ground. Grind the almonds in a food processor with the cornmeal to prevent them from turning into a paste.
2. See page 153 for the recipe for candied orange peel, or see page 154 for a source.

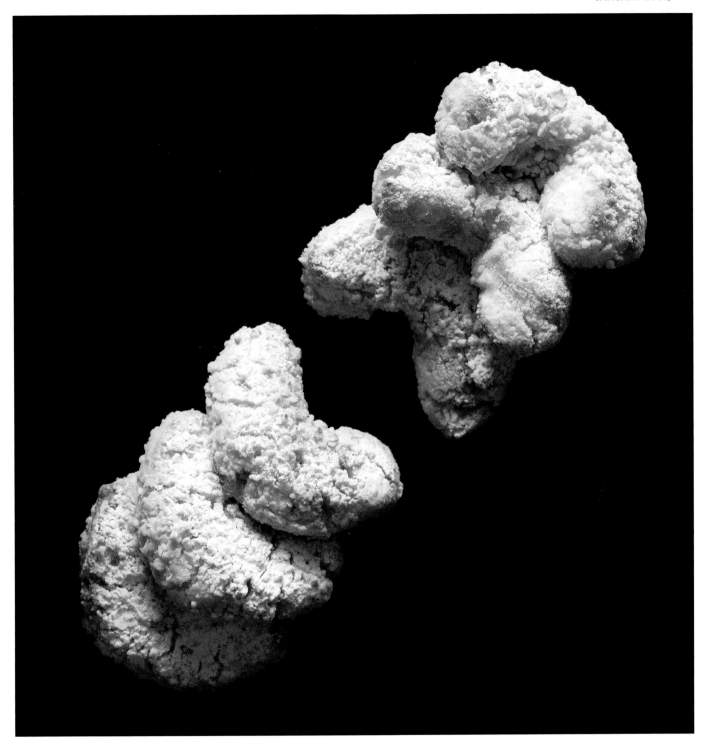

1990s

In the nineties, food became a serious part of American popular culture. During the decade of the celebrity chef, cookies underwent a sea change as well, as Americans went back to their roots, seeking out great American cookies and traveling abroad to hunt down new flavors. The search for the new led to a craze for biscotti. Impossible though it may sound, cookies became richer than ever: now recipes called not for just any old chocolate, but for fine chocolate.

MOCHA COOKIES

The nineties were the chocolate decade in America. This recipe—from the Bakery on Melrose Avenue in Los Angeles—has no subtlety: it revels in its rich chocolate decadence. The fact that it is remarkably easy to put together is a bonus. You begin with melted chocolate, a ton of chocolate chips, and a spot of espresso powder—and you end up with a cookie that everybody adores. Make these cookies once, and you'll be making them for the rest of your life.

MAKES ABOUT 3 DOZEN COOKIES

- 4 ounces unsweetened chocolate, chopped
- 3 cups semisweet chocolate chips
- 1 stick (½ cup) unsalted butter, cut into bits
- ½ cup all-purpose flour
- ½ teaspoon double-acting baking powder
- ½ teaspoon salt
- 4 large eggs, at room temperature
- 1½ cups sugar
- 1½ tablespoons instant espresso powder
- 2 teaspoons vanilla

In a metal bowl set over a saucepan of simmering water, melt the unsweetened chocolate, 1½ cups of the chocolate chips, and the butter, stirring until the mixture is smooth, and remove the bowl from the heat. In a small bowl, stir together the flour, the baking powder, and the salt. In a bowl, beat the eggs with the sugar until the mixture is thick and pale, and beat in the espresso powder and the vanilla. Fold the chocolate mixture into the egg mixture, fold in the flour mixture, and stir in the remaining 1½ cups chocolate chips. Let the batter stand for 15 minutes. Drop the batter by heaping tablespoons onto baking sheets lined with parchment paper and bake the cookies in the middle of a preheated 350°F oven for 8 to 10 minutes, or until they are puffed and shiny and cracked on top. Let the cookies cool on the baking sheets, transfer them to racks, and let them cool completely.

RECIPE NOTES
1. Err on the side of underbaking these cookies. They are meant to be soft and rich.
2. Cool for 1 minute on the baking sheet before transferring the cookies to racks.

JAN HAGELS
(CINNAMON ALMOND WAFERS)

Americans adapted the word "cookie" from the Dutch *koekje*. In one article in the magazine, the authors offered a dozen very special Dutch cookies, from "little Fresian thumbs" to "girls from Arnheim" and "bricks from Weesp." You'll be delighted to make the acquaintance of these "Hail Johns." Crisp and buttery, each one is topped with sliced almonds and a sprinkling of cinnamon sugar.

MAKES 50 WAFERS

1¾ sticks (¾ cup plus 2 tablespoons) unsalted butter, softened
½ cup firmly packed light brown sugar
1 teaspoon grated fresh lemon zest
1 large egg, beaten lightly
2⅓ cups all-purpose flour
⅔ cup sliced almonds
2 tablespoons granulated sugar
1 teaspoon ground cinnamon

In a bowl with an electric mixer, cream the butter with the brown sugar, the zest, and 1 tablespoon of the egg until the mixture is light and fluffy, and stir in the flour. On a lightly buttered baking sheet, pat the dough into a 14-by-10-inch rectangle, brush it with the remaining egg, and sprinkle it evenly with the almonds. In a small bowl, stir together the granulated sugar and the cinnamon and sprinkle the mixture evenly over the almonds. Bake the pastry in the middle of a preheated 350°F oven for 20 to 25 minutes, or until it is golden, and while it is still hot, cut it into 2-by-1-inch wafers. Transfer the wafers to racks and let them cool.

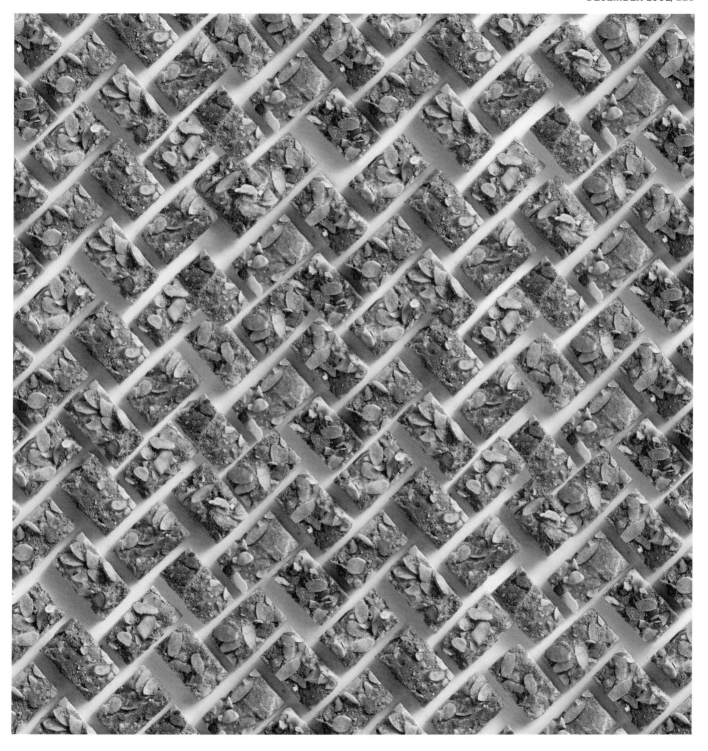

CRANBERRY PISTACHIO BISCOTTI

"Are biscotti the cookies of the '90s?" asked the baking authority Carol Field. "It seems that these traditional crunchy, nut-filled Italian cookies can be found everywhere today." Indeed, the country went mad for biscotti, making them in every possible permutation. Over the years, we have printed dozens of different recipes but this one is, hands-down, our favorite. The combination of chewy, sweet-sour bits of cranberries and nuts within a very crunchy cookie is only part of their appeal; they are also extremely pretty.

MAKES ABOUT 3 DOZEN BISCOTTI

1⅓ cups (about ¼ pound) dried cranberries (available at specialty food stores and some supermarkets)
2½ cups unbleached all-purpose flour
1 cup sugar
½ teaspoon baking soda
½ teaspoon double-acting baking powder
½ teaspoon salt
3 large eggs
1 teaspoon vanilla
1 cup shelled natural pistachio nuts
An egg wash made by beating together 1 large egg and 1 teaspoon water

In a bowl, combine the cranberries with enough hot water to cover them and let them soak for 5 minutes. Drain the cranberries well and pat them dry with paper towels. In the bowl of an electric mixer fitted with the paddle attachment, blend the flour, the sugar, the baking soda, the baking powder, and the salt until the mixture is combined well, add the eggs and the vanilla, beating until a dough is formed, and stir in the cranberries and the pistachios.

→ Turn the dough out onto a lightly floured surface, knead it several times, and halve it. Working on a large buttered and floured baking sheet, with floured hands form each piece of dough into a flattish log 13 inches long and 2 inches wide, arrange the logs at least 3 inches apart on the sheet, and brush them with the egg wash. Bake the logs in the middle of a preheated 325°F oven for 30 minutes, and let them cool on the baking sheet on a rack for 10 minutes. On a cutting board, cut the logs crosswise on the diagonal into ¾-inch-thick slices, arrange the biscotti, cut sides down, on the baking sheet, and bake them in the 325°F oven for 10 to 12 minutes on each side, or until they are pale golden. Transfer the biscotti to racks to cool and store them in airtight containers.

RECIPE NOTES
1. If the only shelled pistachios you can find are salted, lower the amount of salt in the recipe to ¼ teaspoon.
2. You can also use a handheld electric mixer to make the dough.

AUNT SIS'S STRAWBERRY TART COOKIES

Cookies appeared on the cover of *Gourmet* for the first time. And to celebrate the occasion, the magazine published a mini-cookbook of staff recipes. This recipe was contributed by food editor Amy Mastrangelo, then *Gourmet*'s reigning cookie queen. Each Christmas she baked up an assortment for all of her colleagues. "We couldn't wait for them!" remembers an editor. "Each one was perfect." These lovely little thumbprint cookies, each one like a tiny strawberry pie, were always the first to disappear. Bake them, and you'll understand why.

MAKES ABOUT 8 DOZEN COOKIES

- 3 cups all-purpose flour
- 1 cup sugar
- ½ teaspoon salt
- 3 sticks (1½ cups) cold unsalted butter, cut into bits
- 2 large egg yolks, beaten lightly
- 1 cup strained strawberry jam

In a large bowl, whisk together the flour, the sugar, and the salt, add the butter, and blend the mixture until it resembles coarse meal. Stir in the egg yolks, blend the mixture until it forms a dough, and chill the dough, wrapped in plastic wrap, for at least 2 hours, or overnight. → Preheat the oven to 350°F. Let the dough soften slightly, roll level teaspoons of it into balls, and arrange the balls about 2 inches apart on lightly greased baking sheets. Using your thumb, make an indentation in the center of each ball, being careful not to crack the dough around the edges. (If the dough cracks, reroll it and try again.) Fill each indentation with about ¼ teaspoon of the jam and bake the cookies in batches in the middle of the oven for 12 to 15 minutes, or until the edges are pale golden. Let the cookies cool on the sheets for 2 minutes, transfer them to racks, and let them cool completely. The cookies may be made 1 month in advance and kept frozen in airtight containers.

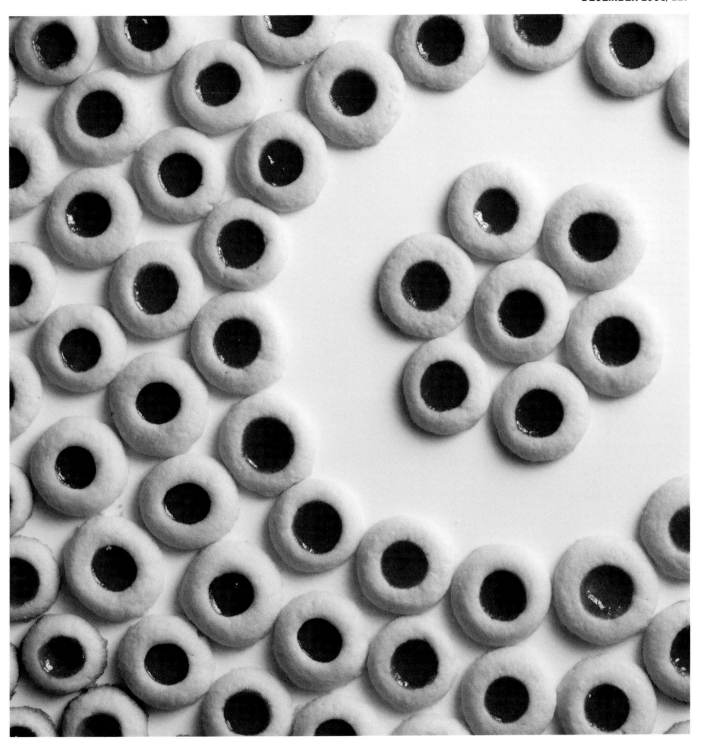

BASLER BRUNSLI (HEART-SHAPED CHOCOLATE ALMOND SPICE COOKIES)

Gourmet's New York restaurant critic devoted an entire column to great chocolate desserts, which shows how strongly the ingredient had captured the American imagination. No wonder that when the renowned pastry chef and teacher Nick Malgieri wrote about his years cooking in Switzerland, he included these chocolate cookies among the *Weihnachtsguetzli* ("Christmas goodies"). With lots of spice and no flour, these bittersweet cookies showcase the chocolate, so use the best that you can find.

MAKES ABOUT 5 DOZEN COOKIES

1½ cups whole natural almonds (8 ounces)
1½ cups sugar, plus additional for coating work surface
  6 ounces Swiss or other fine-quality semisweet or bittersweet chocolate, chopped
1½ teaspoons cinnamon
½ teaspoon ground cloves
¼ cup egg whites (from about 2 large eggs)

In a food processor, combine almonds with 1½ cups sugar and pulse until ground fine (do not overprocess, or mixture will become warm and melt chocolate when added). Add chocolate and pulse until ground fine. Add spices and pulse twice. Add whites and pulse until mixture forms a stiff dough, adding 1 teaspoon water if necessary.

→ Line 2 baking sheets with parchment paper or foil.
→ On a surface coated with additional sugar, press out or roll dough about ¼ inch thick. With bottom of fork held facing down and tines touching dough at 60-degree angle, score dough about ¹⁄₁₆ inch deep by pulling fork across in a series of parallel vertical lines. With a 2-inch heart-, star-, and/or clover-leaf-shaped cutter, cut out cookies and transfer to prepared baking sheets. Press dough scraps together and cut out more cookies in same manner. Let cookies stand, uncovered, at room temperature 3 hours.

→ Preheat oven to 325°F.
→ Put cookies in oven and immediately reduce temperature to 300°F. Bake cookies, switching position of sheets in oven halfway through baking, 10 to 15 minutes, or until they are just firm (do not overbake, or cookies will be hard), and cool on sheets on racks. Keep cookies in an airtight container up to 2 weeks.

RECIPE NOTE
The dough is sticky, so roll it out between sheets of parchment or wax paper, sprinkling the bottom sheet with sugar. Then remove the top sheet, cut out the cookies, and peel them right off the paper.

COCONUT MACADAMIA SHORTBREAD

Macadamia nuts get a bad rap because they are so incredibly rich. But they are also incredibly nutritious, and they have the highest amount of beneficial monounsaturated fats of any nut. So although this combination of macadamia nuts, coconut and butter may sound sinful, think of it as good for you.

MAKES 8 COOKIES

- ½ cup salted macadamia nuts
- 2 tablespoons granulated sugar
- ¾ stick (6 tablespoons) unsalted butter, softened
- ¼ cup confectioners' sugar
- 1 cup cake flour (not self-rising)
- ½ teaspoon baking powder
- ¼ teaspoon salt
- ½ cup plus 1 tablespoon sweetened shredded coconut

Preheat oven to 325°F and generously butter a 9-inch round cake pan.
→ In a food processor, pulse nuts and granulated sugar just until ground fine (do not grind to a paste).
→ In a bowl with an electric mixer, beat butter with confectioners' sugar until light and fluffy. In another bowl, whisk together flour, baking powder, salt, nut mixture, and ¼ cup coconut. Beat flour mixture into butter mixture until just combined.
→ On a lightly floured surface, knead dough 5 to 8 times, or until it just comes together. With floured hands (dough will be sticky) press dough evenly into prepared cake pan and sprinkle with remaining 5 tablespoons coconut, pressing lightly to make it adhere. Bake shortbread in middle of oven 30 minutes, or until pale golden.
→ While shortbread is still warm, loosen edges from pan with a small knife and cut into 8 wedges. Let shortbread cool in pan. Carefully transfer shortbread to a platter.

ANISE-SCENTED FIG AND DATE SWIRLS

Icebox cookies are a boon to any cook. This fruit-filled dough, for instance, can be formed into a log and then put into the refrigerator for a week, or the freezer for a month. Baked, the cookies keep for days. Hard to believe that something so striking can also be so accommodating.

MAKES ABOUT 3 DOZEN COOKIES

- 1 cup firmly packed dried figs (as soft as possible)
- 1 cup firmly packed pitted dates
- ⅓ cup water
- ½ cup plus 2 tablespoons granulated sugar
- 1¾ cups all-purpose flour
- 1 tablespoon ground anise seeds
- ¼ teaspoon baking powder
- ¼ teaspoon baking soda
- ¼ teaspoon salt
- 1 stick (½ cup) unsalted butter, softened
- 4 ounces cream cheese
- 1 teaspoon vanilla
- 1 large egg yolk
- ¼ cup granulated raw sugar (turbinado or Demerara)

In a blender, puree figs and dates with water and 2 tablespoons sugar. In a bowl, whisk together flour, anise, baking powder, baking soda, and salt. In another bowl with an electric mixer, beat together butter, cream cheese, and remaining ½ cup sugar until light and fluffy. Add vanilla, yolk, and flour mixture and beat until a dough forms. Form dough into a disk. Chill dough, wrapped in wax paper, 1 hour, or until firm enough to handle.

→ On a lightly floured sheet of wax paper, with a floured rolling pin, roll out dough into a 13-by-10-inch rectangle, about ⅓ inch thick. Drop fig mixture by spoonfuls onto dough and gently spread in an even layer over dough. Starting with a long side, roll dough jelly-roll fashion into a 13-inch log, using wax paper as an aid. Roll log in raw sugar to coat. Chill log, wrapped in wax paper, 4 hours, or until firm enough to handle.

→ Preheat oven to 350°F and lightly butter 2 baking sheets.

→ Cut log into ⅓-inch-thick rounds and arrange about 2 inches apart on baking sheets. Bake cookies in batches in middle of oven until pale golden, about 13 minutes, and transfer to racks to cool.

RECIPE NOTES

1. Trim the stems from the figs before pureeing them.
2. Use a food processor to puree the figs and dates.
3. If the dough becomes too soft while rolling, chill it until it is firm.
4. Leave a ¼-inch border when spreading the filling.

CHOCOLATE COCONUT SQUARES

Gourmet published dozens of different cookie recipes in 1997—a dozen in this issue alone. So why did we choose this as the best of the year? For one thing, because it is so easy: the cookie begins with a base of cracker crumbs mixed with coconut and butter. But then comes the remarkable part: in the nineties, we discovered how easy it is to make ganache. In this case, you mix just three ingredients to create a dense, silky smooth layer of chocolate. You end up with an irresistible treat that falls somewhere between a bar cookie and a candy bar. It may be possible to find someone who doesn't like this, but we have yet to meet that person.

MAKES 3 DOZEN SQUARES

13 small (2-inch) wheatmeal biscuits, such as Carr's,
     or ten 5-by-2½-inch graham crackers
¾ stick (6 tablespoons) unsalted butter
2 cups sweetened flaked coconut (about 5 ounces)
¼ teaspoon salt
12 ounces fine-quality bittersweet chocolate (not unsweetened)
2 large egg yolks
1 cup heavy cream
    Confectioners' sugar for dusting

Preheat oven to 350°F.
→ In a food processor, pulse biscuits or crackers until finely ground. Melt butter and in large bowl, stir together with crumbs, coconut, and salt until combined. Firmly press crumb mixture evenly onto bottom of a 9-inch square baking pan and bake in middle of oven until golden, about 15 minutes. Cool crust completely in pan on a rack.
→ Chop chocolate. In a double boiler or a metal bowl set over a saucepan of barely simmering water, melt chocolate, stirring until smooth. Remove top of double boiler or bowl from heat and cool chocolate 15 minutes.

→ In a small bowl, lightly beat yolks. In a saucepan, heat cream over moderate heat until it just boils and whisk ½ cup into yolks, whisking constantly. Add mixture to remaining cream and cook over moderate heat, whisking, until an instant-read thermometer registers 160°F. Whisk custard into chocolate until just smooth and pour evenly over crust, smoothing top with a small metal offset spatula or rubber spatula. Chill confection, covered, at least 4 hours, or until firm.
→ With a sharp thin knife, cut confection into 36 squares. Squares keep, layered between sheets of wax paper in an airtight container and chilled, 1 week.
→ Using star shapes cut out of parchment paper as a stencil, dust squares with confectioners' sugar.

RECIPE NOTES
1. Butter the baking pan, line it with two crisscrossed sheets of foil, and butter the foil.
2. The star-shaped stencils and confectioners' sugar dusting are purely for decoration; the bars are still elegant when unadorned.

GIANDUIA BROWNIES

Still in thrall to the national chocolate obsession, in 1998 *Gourmet* decided to investigate gianduia. "In the early nineteenth century," wrote author Carole Bloom, "naval blockades imposed by the English against Napoleon sharply curtailed the cacao supplies arriving to continental Europe from the Americas. To avoid using too much of the now-scarce ingredient, the confectioners of Piedmont (then under French occupation) added finely ground hazelnuts to their chocolate." The result was gianduia (zhahn-*doo*-yah), and the world has been a better place ever since. These are the best brownies you will ever taste.

MAKES 16 BROWNIES

1¼ cups hazelnuts (about 6¼ ounces)
4 ounces fine-quality bittersweet chocolate (not unsweetened)
3 ounces fine-quality milk chocolate
1 stick (½ cup) unsalted butter
¼ cup Nutella (chocolate-hazelnut spread)
½ cup all-purpose flour
½ teaspoon baking powder
½ cup sugar
2 large eggs

Preheat oven to 350°F and butter and flour a 9-inch square baking pan, knocking out excess flour,

→ Toast and skin hazelnuts. In a food processor, pulse hazelnuts until coarsely ground (bits should be about ⅛ inch).

→ Chop chocolates into small pieces and, in a double boiler or a metal bowl set over a saucepan of barely simmering water, melt chocolates with butter and Nutella, stirring occasionally until smooth. Remove top of double boiler or bowl from heat.

→ While chocolates are melting, into a bowl, sift together flour, baking powder, and a pinch salt. Whisk sugar into chocolate mixture until combined well. Add eggs, whisking until mixture is glossy and smooth. Stir in flour mixture and hazelnuts until just combined.

→ Pour batter into baking pan and bake in middle of oven 35 to 40 minutes, or until a tester comes out with moist crumbs adhering to it. Cool brownies completely in pan on a rack and cut into 16 squares.

→ Brownies keep, layered between sheets of wax paper in an airtight container at cool room temperature, 5 days.

RECIPE NOTES

1. Butter the baking pan, line it with two crisscrossed sheets of foil, and butter the foil.

2. Toast the hazelnuts in a preheated 350°F oven for 10 to 15 minutes, or until the nuts are lightly colored and the skins are blistered. Wrap the nuts in a kitchen towel and steam for 1 minute; then rub them in the towel to remove the loose skins. Cool completely before grinding.

SKIBO CASTLE GINGER CRUNCH

Once again the recipe format underwent a transformation. In 1999, *Gourmet* took pity on time-challenged readers and began to tell them how long it was going to take them to cook each dish in the magazine. These British cookies contributed by an Irish reader who had been a cook in Scotland require remarkably little labor. Contribute a mere 15 minutes of your time, and you will be rewarded with a crisp, grown-up little cookie that one reader described as "magical."

MAKES 64 COOKIES
ACTIVE TIME: 15 MIN
START TO FINISH: 1¾ HR

FOR SHORTBREAD BASE
- 1¼ cups all-purpose flour
- 3 tablespoons granulated sugar
- 1 teaspoon baking powder
- 1 teaspoon ground ginger
- ¼ teaspoon salt
- 1 stick (½ cup) cold unsalted butter, cut into pieces

FOR TOPPING
- ¾ stick (6 tablespoons) unsalted butter
- 1 tablespoon Lyle's Golden Syrup (British cane sugar syrup; see Sources, page 154)
- 1 cup confectioners' sugar
- ½ teaspoon ground ginger
- ½ teaspoon vanilla

Preheat oven to 350°F and grease a 13-by-9-inch metal baking pan.

MAKE SHORTBREAD BASE: Sift together dry ingredients and blend in butter with your fingertips until mixture resembles coarse meal. Press evenly into bottom of pan (base will be thin). Bake in middle of oven until golden and crisp, 20 to 25 minutes.

MAKE TOPPING JUST BEFORE SHORTBREAD IS DONE: Melt butter in a small saucepan and whisk in remaining ingredients until smooth. Bring to a boil and simmer, stirring, 30 seconds.

POUR TOPPING: Remove shortbread from oven and pour topping over, tilting pan to cover shortbread evenly. Cool in pan on a rack, then cut into small rectangles (8 rows lengthwise and 8 crosswise).

RECIPE NOTE
For larger cookies, cut into 4 rows lengthwise and 9 crosswise.

2000s

This has been a stellar cookie decade; during the year 2000, *Gourmet* published as many cookie recipes as it had in the first ten years of its existence. What you can't help noticing is the attempt at innovation. If recipes are classics, they are given a twist: they are smaller, they contain an unusual ingredient, or require a new technique. But as the decade comes to a close, the cookies take off in new directions, becoming utterly original.

WALNUT ACORN COOKIES

Cookies had become such an important part of *Gourmet's* holiday repertoire that the editors started asking readers to contribute their favorite recipes—and they poured into the magazine's kitchens in such profusion that it was difficult to choose among them. But to our mind, this beautiful, buttery little cookie is the best of a very fine lot. With little effort, you end up with a cookie that looks as if it came from a professional bakery—while possessing the rich, nutty flavor of home-baked pastry.

MAKES ABOUT 4 DOZEN COOKIES
ACTIVE TIME: 1½ HOURS
START TO FINISH: 2½ HOURS

FOR COOKIES
2 cups all-purpose flour
½ teaspoon baking powder
¼ teaspoon salt
2 sticks (1 cup) unsalted butter, melted and cooled
¾ cup packed light brown sugar
1 teaspoon vanilla
1 cup finely chopped walnuts (4 ounces)

FOR DECORATION
8 ounces semisweet chocolate, melted
½ cup finely chopped walnuts (2 ounces)

MAKE COOKIES: Sift together flour, baking powder, and salt. Beat together butter, brown sugar, and vanilla with an electric mixer until pale and fluffy. Mix in flour mixture at low speed, then stir in walnuts.
→ Preheat oven to 375°F.
→ Form 2 teaspoons dough into an egglike shape the size of an acorn. Make more "acorns," arranging them 1 inch apart on ungreased baking sheets. Bake in batches in middle of oven until undersides are light brown, about 10 minutes. Transfer to racks to cool.
DECORATE COOKIES: Dip half of each cookie in melted chocolate and then in chopped nuts. Place as coated on a baking sheet lined with wax paper to set, about 15 minutes.

RECIPE NOTE
The cookies keep, layered between sheets of wax paper, for up to 1 week.

CRANBERRY TURTLE BARS

Beautiful, tart cranberries contain a great deal of natural pectin. That quality means that when they are mixed with sugar and pecans and set onto a buttery crust, they turn into a wonderful candied topping. Add a few chocolate streaks, and it's easy to understand why this cookie has gained such a passionate following. It's an unexpected—and unexpectedly delicious—combination.

MAKES 3 DOZEN BARS
ACTIVE TIME: 30 MINUTES
START TO FINISH: 2 HOURS

FOR BASE
2 cups all-purpose flour
½ cup packed light brown sugar
½ teaspoon salt
1½ sticks (¾ cup) cold unsalted butter, cut into ½-inch cubes

FOR TOPPING
2 sticks (1 cup) unsalted butter
1⅔ cups granulated sugar
¼ cup light corn syrup
½ teaspoon salt
1½ cups fresh or frozen cranberries (not thawed; 6¾ ounces), coarsely chopped
1 teaspoon vanilla
3 cups pecans (12 ounces), toasted and cooled, then coarsely chopped

FOR DECORATION
2 ounces fine-quality bittersweet chocolate (not unsweetened), very finely chopped

SPECIAL EQUIPMENT: a candy thermometer

MAKE BASE: Preheat oven to 350°F.
→ Line a 15-by-10-inch shallow baking pan (1 inch deep) with foil, leaving a 2-inch overhang on the 2 short sides. Butter all 4 sides (but not bottom).
→ Blend flour, brown sugar, and salt in a food processor, then add butter and pulse until mixture begins to form small (roughly pea-size) lumps. Sprinkle into baking pan, then press down firmly all over with a metal spatula to form an even layer. Bake in middle of oven until golden and firm to the touch, 15 to 17 minutes, then cool in pan on a rack.

MAKE TOPPING: Melt butter in a 3-quart heavy saucepan over moderate heat and stir in sugar, corn syrup, and salt. Boil over moderately high heat, stirring occasionally, until caramel registers 245°F on thermometer, about 8 minutes. Carefully stir in cranberries, then boil until caramel returns to 245°F. Remove from heat and stir in vanilla, then stir in pecans until well coated. Working quickly, spread caramel topping over base, using a fork to distribute nuts and berries evenly. Cool completely.

CUT AND DECORATE BARS: Lift bars in foil from pan and transfer to a cutting board. Cut into 6 crosswise strips, then 6 lengthwise strips to form 36 bars.
→ Melt half of chocolate in top of a double boiler or a metal bowl set over a saucepan of barely simmering water, stirring until smooth. Remove bowl from heat and add remaining chocolate, stirring until smooth. Transfer chocolate to a small heavy-duty sealable plastic bag. Seal bag and snip off a tiny piece of 1 corner to form a small hole, then pipe chocolate decoratively over bars. Let stand at room temperature until chocolate sets, about 1 hour.

RECIPE NOTES
1. Use a small offset metal spatula to spread the cranberry mixture.
2. Rather than cutting them first, decorate the bars and let the chocolate set before cutting.
3. For larger bars, cut into 6 rows lengthwise and 4 crosswise.
4. The bars keep in an airtight container (use wax paper between the layers) for up to 1 week.

SCANDINAVIAN ROSETTES

You begin with a classic crepe batter, and with the help of a rosette iron, you create these extraordinary cookies, as lovely as butterflies and every bit as light. Reach for one, and you won't believe how ethereal they are, how little they weigh. Take a bite, and you will be startled by the sound of the crunch.

MAKES ABOUT 3 DOZEN COOKIES
ACTIVE TIME: 1¼ HOURS
START TO FINISH: 1¼ HOURS

- 2 large eggs
- 2 tablespoons granulated sugar
- 1 cup whole milk
- 1 teaspoon vanilla
- 1 cup all-purpose flour
- ¼ teaspoon salt
- 1½ quarts vegetable oil
- ¼ cup confectioners' sugar

SPECIAL EQUIPMENT: a rosette iron

Whisk together eggs, granulated sugar, milk, and vanilla in a large bowl, then add flour and salt, whisking until combined.

→ Heat oil in a 3- to 4-quart heavy saucepan with rosette iron in it until thermometer registers 370° to 375°F. Carefully lift out iron, letting oil drip off into pan. Dip all but top edge of iron into batter 3 seconds, then submerge iron in oil and fry (batter adhering to iron) until golden, 35 to 40 seconds (do not let go of iron; cookie will shatter if it hits bottom of saucepan). Lift out iron, letting oil drip off, and, working over paper towels, carefully pry off rosette with a fork. Let rosette drain, hollow side down, on paper towels, then make more rosettes in same manner, heating iron in oil 10 seconds before dipping it into batter each time.

→ Dust rosettes with confectioners' sugar before serving.

RECIPE NOTES
1. To order a rosette iron, see Sources (page 154).
2. This recipe can be easily halved.
3. The rosettes are best eaten within 1 day of being made, but they can be kept, layered between sheets of wax paper or parchment paper, in an airtight container at room temperature for up to 2 days.

BISCOTTI QUADRATI AL MIELE E ALLE NOCI (HONEY NUT SQUARES)

When *Gourmet* devoted an entire issue to the wonders of Rome, it was filled with authentic and irresistible food from classic fried artichokes to fettuccine Alfredo and pizza bianca. Romans may not have a large dessert repertoire, but they make up for it with this incredible and classic cookie: almonds, hazelnuts, and pine nuts suspended in honey and cream and set on a buttery crust. It is a bit of glossy goodness.

MAKES 25 (1-INCH) BARS
ACTIVE TIME: 30 MINUTES
START TO FINISH: 2 HOURS

FOR CRUST
1¼ cups all-purpose flour
2 tablespoons sugar
½ teaspoon baking powder
¼ teaspoon salt
1 stick (½ cup) cold unsalted butter, cut into pieces
1 large egg, lightly beaten

FOR TOPPING
⅓ cup plus 1 tablespoon mild honey
¼ cup packed light brown sugar
⅛ teaspoon salt
3 tablespoons cold unsalted butter, cut into pieces
1 tablespoon heavy cream
½ cup whole almonds with skins (3 ounces), toasted
¾ cup hazelnuts (4 ounces), toasted and any loose skins rubbed off in a kitchen towel
¼ cup pine nuts (1½ ounces), lightly toasted

SPECIAL EQUIPMENT: a pastry or bench scraper

MAKE CRUST: Butter a 9-inch square metal baking pan (2 inches deep) and line with 2 crisscrossed sheets of foil, leaving a 2-inch overhang on all sides. Butter foil.

→ Blend together flour, sugar, baking powder, salt, and butter with your fingertips or a pastry blender (or pulse in a food processor) until most of mixture resembles coarse meal with small (roughly pea-size) butter lumps. Add egg and stir with a fork (or pulse) until a crumbly dough forms.
→ Turn out dough onto a work surface and divide into 4 portions. With heel of your hand, smear each portion once or twice in a forward motion to help distribute fat. Gather dough together with scraper.
→ Preheat oven to 375°F.
→ Press dough evenly onto bottom (but not up sides) of baking pan and bake in middle of oven until edges are golden and begin to pull away from sides of pan, 15 to 20 minutes. Cool in pan on rack.
MAKE TOPPING: Bring honey, brown sugar, and salt to a boil in a 2-quart heavy saucepan over moderate heat, stirring until sugar is dissolved, then boil, without stirring, 2 minutes. Add butter and cream and boil, stirring, 1 minute. Remove from heat and stir in all nuts until completely coated.
→ Pour nut mixture over pastry crust, spreading evenly, and bake in middle of oven until topping is caramelized and bubbling, 12 to 15 minutes. Cool completely in pan on a rack. Lift out of pan using foil overhang and cut into 25 squares.

RECIPE NOTE
The honey nut squares keep, layered between sheets of wax paper, in an airtight container at room temperature for up to 1 week.

POLISH APRICOT-FILLED COOKIES

Readers once again responded to a plea for family recipes. This one, from Frederika Schwanka, of Terryville, Connecticut, is notable for the tenderness of the cream cheese pastry and the tanginess of the filling.

MAKES ABOUT 5 DOZEN COOKIES
ACTIVE TIME: 1½ HOURS
START TO FINISH: 4 HOURS (INCLUDES CHILLING)

FOR PASTRY DOUGH
2¼ cups all-purpose flour
½ teaspoon salt
8 ounces cream cheese, softened
2 sticks (1 cup) unsalted butter, softened
1 large egg, lightly beaten with 2 teaspoons water for egg wash

FOR APRICOT FILLING
1¾ cups coarsely chopped dried apricots (10 ounces)
½ cup golden raisins
⅔ cup mild honey
¼ cup sweet orange marmalade
½ teaspoon cinnamon
1 cup water

SPECIAL EQUIPMENT: parchment paper
GARNISH: confectioners' sugar

MAKE DOUGH: Whisk together flour and salt in a bowl until combined. Beat cream cheese and butter in a large bowl with an electric mixer at medium-high speed until pale and creamy, about 3 minutes in a stand mixer (preferably fitted with a paddle attachment) or 6 minutes with a handheld. Reduce mixer speed to low, then add flour mixture and mix just until combined.
→ Divide dough into 4 equal pieces and wrap each in plastic wrap. Chill until firm, about 1½ hours.
MAKE FILLING WHILE PASTRY CHILLS: Bring apricots, raisins, honey, marmalade, cinnamon, and water to a boil in a 2- to 3-quart heavy saucepan over moderate heat, stirring. Reduce heat and simmer,

stirring, until dried fruit is softened and mixture is thick, about 10 minutes. Transfer to a small bowl and cool until warm, about 20 minutes. Transfer to a food processor and pulse until finely chopped. Chill until cold, about 2 hours.
ASSEMBLE AND BAKE COOKIES: Put oven rack in middle position and preheat oven to 375°F. Line a large baking sheet with parchment.
→ Roll out 1 piece of dough (keep remaining pieces chilled) between 2 (12-inch) sheets of well-floured wax paper with a rolling pin into a roughly 11-inch square. (If dough gets too soft, transfer dough in wax paper to a baking sheet and chill until firm.) Discard top sheet of wax paper and trim dough with a pastry wheel or sharp knife into a 10-inch square. Cut square into 4 equal strips, then cut crosswise in fourths again to form a total of 16 (2½-inch) squares.
→ Working quickly, place 1 heaping teaspoon filling in center of each square. Brush 2 opposite corners with egg wash, then bring corners together and pinch firmly to adhere. (If dough becomes too soft, freeze it on a baking sheet for a few minutes.)
→ Arrange cookies 2 inches apart on baking sheet. Bake until golden, 17 to 20 minutes, then transfer with a metal spatula to racks to cool completely. Make more cookies with remaining dough and filling on a lined cool baking sheet.

RECIPE NOTES
1. For the best flavor, we recommend California apricots.
2. The dough is extremely tender; if at any time during the filling process it gets too soft to work with, chill it on wax paper on a large baking sheet.
3. You will have leftover filling, which is wonderful spread on toast.
4. Dust cooled cookies with confectioners' sugar if desired.
5. The cookies keep, layered between sheets of wax paper or parchment, in an airtight container at room temperature for up to 4 days.

MINI BLACK AND WHITE COOKIES

If you have ever lived in New York City, you have a natural affinity for the giant black-and-white cookies that are sold in every grocery and deli. More mini-cake than cookie, they are frosted with sweet half-moons of icing, chocolate on one half, vanilla on the other. Most people find themselves taking a bite here and a bite there, trying to decide which side is more delicious. We shrank the cookies down to dainty tidbits, just to make restraint a little easier.

MAKES ABOUT 5 DOZEN COOKIES
ACTIVE TIME: 1 HOUR
START TO FINISH: 1½ HOURS

FOR COOKIES
1¼ cups all-purpose flour
½ teaspoon baking soda
½ teaspoon salt
⅓ cup well-shaken buttermilk
½ teaspoon vanilla
7 tablespoons unsalted butter, softened
½ cup granulated sugar
1 large egg

FOR ICINGS
2¾ cups confectioners' sugar
2 tablespoons light corn syrup
2 teaspoons fresh lemon juice
½ teaspoon vanilla
4 to 6 tablespoons water
¼ cup unsweetened Dutch-process cocoa powder

SPECIAL EQUIPMENT: a small offset spatula

MAKE COOKIES: Put oven racks in upper and lower thirds of oven and preheat oven to 350°F. Butter 2 large baking sheets.
→ Whisk together flour, baking soda, and salt in a bowl. Stir together buttermilk and vanilla in a cup. Beat together butter and sugar in a large bowl with an electric mixer at medium-high speed until pale and fluffy, about 3 minutes, then add egg, beating until combined well. Reduce speed to low and add flour mixture and buttermilk mixture alternately in batches, beginning and ending with flour mixture, and mixing just until smooth. Drop rounded teaspoons of batter 1 inch apart onto baking sheets. Bake, switching positions of sheets halfway through baking, until tops are puffed, edges are pale golden, and cookies spring back when touched, 6 to 8 minutes total. Transfer to a rack to cool.

MAKE ICING WHILE COOKIES COOL: Stir together confectioners' sugar, corn syrup, lemon juice, vanilla, and 2 tablespoons water in a small bowl until smooth. If icing is not easily spreadable, add more water, ½ teaspoon at a time. Transfer half of icing to another bowl and stir in cocoa, adding more water, ½ teaspoon at a time, to thin to same consistency as vanilla icing. Cover surface with a dampened paper towel, then cover bowl with plastic wrap.

ICE COOKIES: With offset spatula, spread white icing over half of flat side, the bottom, of each cookie. Starting with cookies you iced first, spread chocolate icing over other half.

RECIPE NOTES
1. For the most uniform rounds, use a pastry bag with a ½-inch tip and pipe out the dough.
2. Once the icing is dry, the cookies keep, layered between sheets of wax paper or parchment, in an airtight container at room temperature for up to 4 days.

CHOCOLATE PEPPERMINT BAR COOKIES

Could anything taste more like Christmas? These are the best flavors of the season in a single bite. It's as if Santa came down the chimney to discover that a steaming cup of cocoa was waiting for him, along with a candy cane to stir it up.

MAKES 32 (2¼-BY-½-INCH) BARS
ACTIVE TIME: 25 MINUTES
START TO FINISH: 1½ HOURS

- ½ cup all-purpose flour
- ½ cup unsweetened cocoa powder (not Dutch-process)
- 1 teaspoon baking soda
- ½ teaspoon salt
- 1 stick (½ cup) unsalted butter, softened
- ¾ cup packed dark brown sugar
- 1 large egg
- 1 cup semisweet chocolate chips (6 ounces)
- 1 cup coarsely crushed peppermint hard candies (¼ pound)

Put oven rack in middle position and preheat oven to 375°F. Line a 13-by-9-inch metal baking pan with 1 sheet of foil, allowing 2 inches of foil to hang over each end of pan, and butter foil (except overhang).
→ Whisk together flour, cocoa powder, baking soda, and salt in a small bowl. Beat together butter and brown sugar in a large bowl with an electric mixer at high speed until pale and fluffy, about 3 minutes. Beat in egg until combined. Reduce speed to low, then mix in flour mixture until just combined. Stir in chocolate chips and candy. Spread dough evenly in pan and bake until puffed and beginning to pull away from sides of pan, about 20 minutes.
→ Cool completely in pan on a rack, then, lifting with foil, transfer to a cutting board. Cut into bars and lift off foil with a spatula.

RECIPE NOTE
The bars keep in an airtight container at room temperature for up to 3 days.

TRIOS

The classic thumbprint cookie gets a modern makeover. By using three different flavors of jam, you not only offer your guests a variety of tastes, but also create a cookie that looks like a miniature holiday ornament.

MAKES ABOUT 3½ DOZEN COOKIES

2½ cups all-purpose flour
1 teaspoon salt
2 sticks (½ pound) unsalted butter, softened
1 cup sugar
1 large egg
1 teaspoon pure vanilla extract
About 2 tablespoons seedless raspberry jam
About 2 tablespoons apricot preserves
About 2 tablespoons strawberry preserves

SPECIAL EQUIPMENT: a ½-inch-thick wooden spoon handle or dowel

MAKE DOUGH: Whisk together flour and salt. Beat butter and sugar with an electric mixer until very pale and fluffy, about 4 minutes, then beat in egg and vanilla. At low speed, mix in flour mixture in 3 batches just until a dough forms. Divide dough in half and form each piece into a 6-inch disk, then chill, wrapped in plastic wrap, until firm, about 1 hour.

ASSEMBLE AND BAKE COOKIES: Preheat oven to 350°F with rack in middle. Line 2 large baking sheets with parchment paper.
→ Roll each of 3 separate level teaspoons of dough into a ball, then flatten each ball slightly (to 1 inch wide and less than ½ inch thick).

Arrange them in a triangle on baking sheet, with edges touching in center, then make a deep indentation in center of each round with wooden spoon handle. Make more cookies, arranging them 1 inch apart on baking sheets.
→ Fill indentation in each cookie with about ⅛ teaspoon jam (each cookie should have 3 different fillings), avoiding any large pieces of fruit.
→ Bake until cookies are baked through and golden brown on edges, 15 to 20 minutes. Cool on baking sheets 5 minutes, then transfer to racks to cool completely.
→ Bake more batches on cooled baking sheets lined with fresh parchment.

RECIPE NOTES
1. The dough can be chilled for up to 2 days before assembling the cookies.
2. Before filling the cookies, chill them so they hold their shape when baked.
3. The cookies will keep, layered between sheets of parchment, in an airtight container at room temperature for up to 1 week.

GLITTERING LEMON SANDWICH COOKIES

If Santa's elves grew citrus trees, these sparkling lemony bites would surely be among the branches. Our favorite in a year rich with cookies, these adorable little balls look like nothing found in any store. They melt in your mouth, leaving behind a lovely citric freshness. Roll them in brightly colored sanding sugar to make them twinkle like vintage ornaments.

MAKES ABOUT 4 DOZEN SANDWICH COOKIES
ACTIVE TIME: 1½ HOURS
START TO FINISH: 2½ HOURS

FOR COOKIES
1⅓ cups all-purpose flour
⅔ cup cornstarch
¼ teaspoon salt
2 sticks (½ pound) unsalted butter, softened
½ cup confectioners' sugar
1 tablespoon grated lemon zest
1 teaspoon vanilla
White and colored sanding sugars

FOR FILLING
1 cup confectioners' sugar
1 tablespoon grated lemon zest
1 tablespoon fresh lemon juice
2 tablespoons light corn syrup
½ stick (4 tablespoons) unsalted butter, softened

SPECIAL EQUIPMENT: a heavy-duty sealable bag

MAKE COOKIES: Preheat oven to 350°F with rack in middle. Line 2 large baking sheets with parchment paper.
→ Whisk together flour, cornstarch, and salt.
→ Beat together butter and confectioners' sugar with an electric mixer until pale and fluffy, then beat in zest and vanilla. At low speed, mix in flour mixture just until a soft dough forms.
→ Put sanding sugars in different bowls. Roll a scant teaspoon of dough into a ball and drop into sugar, turning to coat. Reshape if necessary and transfer to a baking sheet. Repeat, spacing balls ¾ inch apart, until baking sheet is filled.
→ Bake until tops are slightly cracked but still pale (bottoms will be pale golden), 12 to 15 minutes. Transfer cookies on parchment to a rack to cool completely.
→ Form and bake more cookies on second baking sheet.

MAKE FILLING AND SANDWICH COOKIES: Beat together all filling ingredients in a large bowl with an electric mixer at medium speed until combined well. Transfer to sealable bag and snip off a corner.
→ Turn over half of cookies and pipe about ½ teaspoon filling on flat side of each. Sandwich with remaining cookies, pressing gently.

RECIPE NOTES
1. The sugared dough balls should be chilled for 30 minutes or frozen for 5 to 10 minutes to help preserve their round shape. Keep the sandwiched cookies chilled.
2. The unsandwiched cookies keep, in a metal cookie tin, at a cool room temperature for up to 4 days.

GRAND MARNIER GLAZED PAIN D'ÉPICE COOKIES

Allspice, ginger, cinnamon, and nutmeg are familiar flavors. But when combined with honey and rye flour, they give cookies the depth and allure of *pain d'épices*, the Christmas bread of Dijon, France. Chilling the dough for as long as possible (up to 12 hours) allows the flavors to develop and prevents the cookies from spreading during baking.
An easy glaze adds a sweet veneer and is practical as well; it helps a garnish of candied orange peel to adhere.

MAKES ABOUT 80 COOKIES
ACTIVE TIME: 45 MINUTES
START TO FINISH: 1 DAY
(INCLUDES CHILLING DOUGH; DOES NOT INCLUDE MAKING CANDIED ORANGE PEEL)

FOR COOKIES
1 cup rye flour
¾ cup all-purpose flour
1 teaspoon ground allspice
1 teaspoon ground ginger
¾ teaspoon ground cinnamon
¾ teaspoon grated or ground nutmeg
¾ teaspoon salt
2 sticks unsalted butter, softened
¼ cup granulated sugar
¼ cup packed dark brown sugar
1 tablespoon mild honey
1 teaspoon pure vanilla extract

FOR GLAZE
4 cups confectioners sugar, sifted (after measuring)
1 tablespoon Grand Marnier
¼ cup whole milk
4 teaspoons fresh lemon juice

FOR DECORATING
Candied Orange Peel (see page 153 or Sources, page 154) cut into ¼-inch dice
About ¼ teaspoon edible gold luster dust (optional; see Sources)
About ½ teaspoon vodka

SPECIAL EQUIPMENT: a pastry/pizza wheel; a very small paintbrush (⅛ inch wide; optional)

MAKE COOKIES: Whisk together flours, spices, and salt. Beat together butter, sugars, honey, and vanilla with an electric mixer at medium-high speed until creamy, about 1 minute. At low speed, mix in flour mixture until just combined. (Dough will be sticky.)
→ Put dough in a 1-gallon sealable bag (not one with a pleated bottom) and smooth out with rolling pin, filling bag; alternatively, roll out dough between 2 sheets of parchment paper into a 10-inch square (about ¼ inch thick). Chill dough (still in bag or parchment) on a baking sheet 8 to 12 hours to allow flavors to develop.
→ Preheat oven to 350°F with rack in middle.
→ Cut bag open (or remove top layer of parchment). Trim edges of dough, then cut 20 (½-inch-wide) strips with pastry wheel (use a ruler). Cut each strip crosswise into fourths for a total of 80 cookies. If dough begins to soften, chill or freeze until firm.
→ Transfer abou 30 cookies to to an ungreased baking sheet with a spatula, arranging them 1 inch apart (keep unbaked cookies chilled or frozen). If cookies on sheet are no longer cold, chill or freeze until firm. Bake until edges are several shades darker, 13 to 15 minutes. Cool cookies on sheet 1 minute, then transfer to a rack to cool completely. Repeat with remaining cookies.
MAKE GLAZE: Whisk together all glaze ingredients until smooth.
GLAZE AND DECORATE COOKIES: Tip bowl with glaze on its side (to make the pool of glaze as deep as possible) and put a folded kitchen towel under bowl for support. Dip half of a cookie into glaze to coat on a diagonal (lengthwise), letting excess drip off into bowl, then scrape bottom of cookie on edge of bowl to remove excess glaze. Transfer cookie to a rack set over a baking sheet (to catch any drips). Immediately put a piece of candied orange peel on glazed half of cookie. Repeat with remaining cookies.
→ Put luster dust in a small saucer, then add vodka and stir to moisten. Dot candied peel with luster dust (vodka will evaporate, laeving only dust). Let stand until completely set, about 1 hour.

RECIPE NOTES
1. For the best flavor, use freshly ground whole allspice (grind with a mortar and pestle) and freshly grated nutmeg.
2. Luster dust is nontoxic. However, the FDA recommends that it be used for decorative purposes only. If you want to use a coloring that is entirely safe (though not available in gold), try Crystal Colors (see Sources). The colors are great for kids.
3. The cookies keep, layered between sheets of parchment paper in metal tins, at room temperature for up to 3 days.

THE BASICS

BLUE DECORATIVE ICING

MAKES 3 CUPS

   1 **(1 pound) box confectioners' sugar**
   4 **teaspoons powdered egg whites (not reconstituted), such as
      Just Whites**
   ⅓ **cup water**
   1 **tablespoon fresh lemon juice**
   1 **teaspoon vanilla**
   2 **drops sky blue liquid food color (optional; see Sources)**

      **SPECIAL EQUIPMENT: 3 pastry bags and at least two (¼-inch) plain
      pastry tips**

Beat together all ingredients except blue food color in a large bowl with
an electric mixer at medium speed until just combined, about
1 minute.

→ Increase speed to high and continue to beat until icing holds stiff
peaks, about 3 minutes in a stand mixer or 10 with a handheld.
TO DECORATE COOKIES: Set aside one fourth of white icing in a bowl,
covered.
→ Beat food color into remaining icing. Transfer one fourth of blue icing
to a pastry bag fitted with tip (keep surface of remaining blue icing
covered with a dampened paper towel and then cover bowl with plastic
wrap) and trace the outline of each cookie. Let it dry.
→ Thin remaining blue icing with enough water, ½ teaspoon at a time,
until it's thin enough to flow easily, and transfer it to another pastry bag
fitted with tip. Pipe enough icing onto each cookie to flood the area
inside the outline.
→ Working quickly (to keep flooded icing from drying), thin white icing
with water in same manner as blue and transfer it to third bag fitted
with a tip, then add decorative drops to each cookie. Allow icing to set.

CANDIED ORANGE PEEL

MAKES ABOUT 80 STRIPS
ACTIVE TIME: 1 HOUR
START TO FINISH: 5½ HOURS (INCLUDES DRYING TIME)

  4 navel oranges
1½ cups sugar
¾ cup water

Cut peel, including white pith, from oranges with a sharp knife. Cut peel lengthwise into ¼-inch strips. Reserve fruit for another use.
→ Cover peel with cold water in a 3-quart saucepan and bring slowly to a boil over medium heat. Boil 1 minute, then drain. Repeat boiling and draining 2 more times (this will remove bitterness).
→ Oil a large rack and set over a tray or a sheet of parchment paper. Bring sugar and water (¾ cup) to a boil in a large heavy skillet, stirring until sugar has dissolved. Add peel and boil, stirring, until most of syrup is absorbed and pith is translucent, 20 to 25 minutes.
→ Transfer peel to rack, separating strips with a fork. Let dry, uncovered, at room temperature 8 to 12 hours.

RECIPE NOTES
1. The candied peel keeps in an airtight container at room temperature for up to 1 week.
2. If serving the candied peel on its own, you can toss it in granulated sugar after it dries or dip it in melted chocolate.

SOURCES

CANDIED ORANGE PEEL
ChefShop: www.chefshop.com and Kalustyan's: www.kalustyans.com

CRYSTAL COLORS
www.shopbakersnook.com

EDIBLE GOLD LUSTER DUST
Wilton: www.wilton.com

LYLE'S GOLDEN SYRUP
Amazon: www.amazon.com

PIZZELLE IRON, ROSETTE IRON, AND KRUMKAKE IRON
Fante's Kitchen Wares Shop: www.fantes.com

SKY BLUE FOOD COLORING
Wilton: www.wilton.com

WHITE LILY FLOUR
Southern supermarkets, some specialty foods shops, and direct from White Lily Foods Company: www.whitelily.com

INDEX

Page references in *italic* refer to illustrations.

PERMISSIONS

Grateful acknowledgment is made to the following for permission to print their recipes, which were previously published in *Gourmet*.

APRICOT CHEWS
Myman Cherenson

BASLER BRUNSLI
Nick Malgieri

BENNE WAFERS
Margaret Sprowls

BISCOTTI DI REGINA
Alberta Ralls

BRANDY SNAPS
Mr. Walter Hoobs

CHOCOLATE MERINGUE BISCUITS
Margaret Shakespeare

CORNETTI
Virgilio Mosi

CRANBERRY PISTACHIO BISCOTTI
Carol Field

CRANBERRY TURTLE BARS
Tracey Seaman

GIANDUIA BROWNIES
Carole Bloom

JAN HAGEL
Peter G. Rose and Peter de Jong

MANDELBROT
Juliette Elkon

MOCHA COOKIES
The Bakery, LA

OATMEAL MOLASSES COOKIES
S. Walter Stauffer

PECAN TASSIES
Frances Kreeger

SKIBO CASTLE GINGER CRUNCH
Jane A. Van Pelt

WALNUT ACORN COOKIES
Suzanne Perry